I Remember

VINCE LOMBARDI

Other Books in the I Remember Series

I Remember Arthur Ashe

I Remember Augusta

I Remember Paul "Bear" Bryant

I Remember Joe DiMaggio

I Remember Dale Earnhardt

I Remember Ben Hogan

I Remember Bobby Jones

I Remember Pete Maravich

I Remember Walter Payton

I Remember Payne Stewart

I Remember Jim Valvano

I Remember
VINCE LOMBARDI

*Personal Memories of and Testimonials
to Football's First Super Bowl Championship Coach
As Told by the People and Players Who Knew Him*

MIKE TOWLE

CUMBERLAND HOUSE
NASHVILLE, TENNESSEE

Copyright © 2001 by Michael J. Towle

All rights reserved. Written permission must be secured from the publisher to use or reproduce any part of this work, except for brief quotations in critical reviews or articles.

Published by Cumberland House Publishing, Inc., 431 Harding Industrial Drive, Nashville, TN 37211

Cover design by Gore Studio, Inc.
Text design by Mary Sanford

Library of Congress Cataloging-in-Publication Data

Towle, Mike.
    I remember Vince Lombardi : personal memories of and testimonials to football's first Super Bowl championship coach as told by the people and players who knew him / [compiled and edited by] Mike Towle.
        p.   cm.
    Includes bibliographical references (p.   ) and index.
    ISBN 1-58182-214-6 (alk. paper)
    1. Lombardi, Vince—Anecdotes. 2. Lombardi—Friends and associates.
    3. Football coaches—United States—Biography. I. Towle, Mike.
    GV939.I42 2001   2001037130

Printed in the United States of America

1 2 3 4 5 6 7 8 9 10—05 04 03 02 01

to Holley and Andrew

Contents

	Acknowledgments	**IX**
	Introduction	**XI**
1	**TEACHER, TEACHER**	**3**
2	**WEST POINT**	**25**
3	**LAND OF THE GIANTS**	**65**
4	**GREEN BAY AND BEYOND**	**91**
5	**ASSORTED MEMORIES**	**173**
6	**LOMBARDI SPEAKS OUT**	**203**
	Appendix	**227**
	Lombardi's Game-by-Game	
	NFL Coaching Record	
	Notes	**237**
	Index	**243**

ACKNOWLEDGMENTS

This project would not have been possible without plenty of assistance from those around me as well as others who barely knew me.

First, I thank all the folks who graciously consented to an interview for this book: Vince Lombardi Jr., Joe Lombardi, Tex Schramm, Forrest Gregg, Jim Taylor, Dave Robinson, Boyd Dowler, Red Mack, Lee Remmel, Bob Lilly, Pat Richter, Sam Huff, Dick Nolan, Don Maynard, Ken MacAfee, Herb Rich, Joe Heap, Gil Reich, Bill Chance, Jerry Lodge, Peter Vann, Hardy Stone, Bruce Elmblad, Al Paulekas, Bill Yeoman, Larry Higgins, and Herbert Seidell. A number of these people were instrumental in helping me to network with others on the list.

Several people were indispensable in researching information vital to the completion of this book: They were Joe Dibari at Fordham University sports information, Kristin McCormack and Lee Remmel of the Green Bay Packers public relations staff, the U.S. Military Academy media relations office, L. Budd Thalman at Penn State University, the NFL Alumni Association, the Vanderbilt University sports information office, John Biolo, Pat Breen, and Ken MacAfee Jr.

Susan Tucker, Cherie Hale, and Holley Towle put in many hours helping me to transcribe tapes of all the interviews.

Ron Pitkin and Ed Curtis at Cumberland House helped me through this whole process.

Holley, my wife, and our son, Andrew, were always patient and helpful, as usual, while I spent many hours sequestered working on this book.

Our good friends at Cornerstone Church offered moral support, as did our family and friends in and around Nashville, Dallas, Fort Worth, Vermont, Florida, Georgia, and Pennsylvania.

Finally, I thank Jesus Christ for His unending provisions and protection.

INTRODUCTION

With Vince Lombardi, it was all about realizing what he had meant to us after he was gone. Playing football for Lombardi was a grueling exercise in perseverance, alertness, and being able to take a lot of crud from him. He yelled at people a lot of the time; he drilled them, pounding home the same basic stuff over and over and over, and then a little bit more; he cajoled, he cried, he laughed; and he could make you feel like a million dollars one second and lower than pond scum for the next three days. At the time you played for him or worked with him, you could genuinely hate the guy; it was only after you had long left his presence that you could fathom what wonderful things he had done for you in terms of motivation, priority setting, and just getting by and succeeding in life.

There are trophies named after him: One goes to college football's best lineman every year, and another awarded to the team that wins the Super Bowl. Lombardi's Green Bay Packers won the first two Super Bowls ever played, over the Kansas City Chiefs in January 1967 and a year later over the Oakland Raiders. Those two games were the beginning of a new era in professional football, and the twilight of another as those were the last two titles that a Lombardi-coached team would ever win. He quit coaching in 1968, came back to coaching in 1969 with the Washington Redskins, and then died from cancer in early September 1970 at the relatively young age of fifty-seven. He left us more than thirty years ago, but his legacy and his image live on, even if it's comedian Jerry Stiller doing an uncanny impersonation of Lombardi in a television commercial.

A number of books about Lombardi have been written, including at least two biographies, by Michael O'Brien and David Maraniss, that do justice in expertly investigating the details of Lombardi's life. This book, *I Remember Vince Lombardi*, is not intended to be yet another comprehensive biography; it is a collection of verbal snapshots of Lombardi's life, his work habits, and his personality, told, in their words, by dozens of people who knew him best. Some of the men interviewed for this book, including those who went on to become career military officers and corporate CEOs, sometimes had to pause while talking about Lombardi, their voices choked with the knowledge and gratefulness for the difference the coach had made in their lives. In many cases, it wasn't until years after they had been associated with Lombardi that they were able to embrace him in a way that hadn't seemed possible or even appropriate decades earlier.

I Remember

VINCE LOMBARDI

TEACHER, TEACHER

Vince Lombardi served an apprenticeship of twenty years before he became a head football coach beyond the high school level. He was nearly forty-six years old when he got the top job with the Green Bay Packers in 1959. Such a career track is practically unheard-of these days. Today's game of head-coaching musical chairs is pretty much a young man's game.

Many coaches call themselves *teacher* even though they've never stood in front of a classroom full of indifferent teenagers. Their teaching is all done within the framework of a football field and film room.

Lombardi knew the classroom. He toiled for eight years as a teacher-coach at Saint Cecilia's (nicknamed Saints) in Englewood, New Jersey, before he returned to Fordham in 1947 to serve as a football assistant under Ed Danowski. At Saints, Lombardi essentially was a classroom teacher as much as he was a gridiron teacher. Lombardi probably didn't have serious aspirations to be a pro football coach during those years. He liked teaching, and he was good at it. He tried to get even better, enrolling at Seton Hall for additional college courses that would make him a better teacher.

Lombardi's subjects: physics, chemistry, and life. Football—and basketball—entered into his curriculum, but those were extracurricular activities. He was an effective teacher and an enthusiastic one, given to the same football-field-like outbursts of passion when a student dozed off in his classroom, or screwed around, or didn't complete a homework assignment. This wasn't a jock coach going through the motions of honoring a contractual job description. If you were one of Lombardi's students or players, you were there to learn.

Students enrolled in one of Lombardi's classes learned all about the motivational power of fear. They learned discipline, and they soaked up academic knowledge under Lombardi, who had a knack for presenting lessons in such a way as to be easily understood and committed to memory. He was a teacher, and a damn good one, who also happened to coach football. And he did that very, very well, too. Many coaches call themselves teachers, and we all sort of chuckle and go along with that. It was no joke with Lombardi, and the students and players he touched—from Saints all the way through to the Green Bay Packers and Washington Redskins—were sold. As great a salesman as Lombardi was, he was an even better teacher.

Joe Lombardi, now in his seventies and still doing some sales work for a company that sells artificial turf, paints a picture of life at Saints in the forties, with his brother as coach and teacher:

Saints was a small school of only about five hundred students, of which about a hundred, maybe, were boys. If you played football, you usually also played baseball and basketball, and Vince taught more sports than just football. He was the baseball coach, the basketball coach, and the football coach. I didn't play basketball for him, though. I wasn't a basketball player. Football was the only sport I played.

He was attuned to everything: He didn't miss a detail. But that was his character. That was Vince Lombardi. We were state champions three years in a row. Practice was about an hour long, maybe longer. We worked hard out there. We went through our calisthenics, our drills, our scrimmages. He worked with us individually, especially the linemen. We didn't have a blocking sled, so we would have to block him. Oh, yeah. He took on every football player every day. Line up and go after him just like he was a blocking sled, and he was pretty tough. That was a normal day. I didn't know it any other way.

*Father **Timothy Moore**, athletic director at Saint Cecilia's starting in 1942, shared a two-desk office in their cramped quarters:*

He would often say, "Tim, I want to go to confession." He would kneel down beside my desk then and I would hear his confession.[1]

Joe Lombardi *was no longer the cuddly baby brother when Vince went to Saints to teach and coach. Joe, by then, was an almost fully grown teenager now playing football at Saints:*

I played for him at Saints. It was tough playing for him, as a brother. He taught chemistry and physics, and was always the football coach. It wasn't easy. I was a co-captain of the football team and played guard. You never could do anything right for him, although I have some good memories of playing for those championship teams. I think he was tougher on me than he was on the other players because I was his brother. But he was an excellent teacher. He gave good assignments. His classes were active and he made everybody participate in his classes. Even in chemistry class: If one person was doing an experiment, everyone else had to stand around that student and watch. He was right there, too, just to make sure you did it right and to correct you if you needed correction. He was a brilliant guy—he had graduated cum laude from college.

Larry Higgins got a double dose of Lombardi, first as a player at Saints and then as a player at Fordham:

I played football under Lombardi my junior and senior years at Saints. I say junior year, although I couldn't play much at all that year because I had transferred from another school and Lombardi had made a commitment to other guys already there. I was about thirty pounds heavier and much faster than the starting fullback, but I had to sit on the bench my whole junior year. Lombardi told me, "I'll make it up to you, Larry, in your senior year. Believe me, I know you want to play football, but I just can't demoralize the team." So I said, "Okay, I guess I can't do anything about it," so I didn't play much in my junior year. But my senior year I played varsity and that was a year we won the Catholic state championship.

Even though he wouldn't play me much my junior year, we seemed to hit it off so well because we both were very dedicated to the game.

Higgins remembers having the honor of being one of a number of high school players to accompany Lombardi to the Downtown Athletic Club's Heisman Trophy banquet in 1946. It was there that Higgins saw Lombardi at his best—outraged, righteously indignant, and exemplary all at the same time:

I had been picked that year to an area All-Metropolitan Team that included star players from high schools in New York, Connecticut, and New Jersey. I'm not sure why I was included, even though I had set a scoring record for Bergen County that still stands, as far as I know. Perhaps Lombardi had picked me. I don't know. All I know is that I was a part of a great moment in life.

There were eight of us, coaches and players, sitting at a table. Each table had a seat reserved for a sponsor, a wealthy man who had sponsored a table, but our chair was empty when we all sat down. I was seated right next to Coach Lombardi, with the empty seat in between us. Well, our sponsor finally arrives, carrying this big ol' Scotch and water. He was potted—completely drunk. Now, keep in mind that Lombardi was still "just" a high school coach at the time, pretty much an unknown, at least at the Downtown Athletic Club.

This old guy, who's blotto, starts philosophizing about why he was such a big success. At one point he held up the Scotch and he's talking to me for whatever reason; maybe because he couldn't see farther than where I was sitting.

He says, "Kid, this is what made me famous. This drink. I was a nothing salesman until I started to drink, and I got so many friends through drinking that I started to become a terrific salesman."

I looked over at Lombardi and could see him doing a slow boil. Finally, he couldn't take it anymore, and this is where my admiration for the guy was solidified. Here he was in unfamiliar territory about to blow his top. Bigwigs everywhere. Coach Lombardi finally says to the guy, "How dare you to tell a young football player a thing like that, to encourage him to have a life of drinking!" He really laced into this guy, and the man just looked at him, said, "Ah, go to hell," and he got up and walked away and we never saw him back the rest of the night. Driving home that night I really told Coach Lombardi how that had been a wonderful thing to do. It took a lot of guts for him to do that. He stood his ground.

John DeGasperis, a Saint Cecilia's High School football player under Lombardi, had plenty of chances to see Lombardi at his ruthless best (or worst):

We had a tackle named Norval Dobbs at Saint Cecilia's who had eleven boils under his arm. Coach looked at the boils, put some ointment on them, and had Norval ready for practice. At one point during a tough block, Norval let out a scream. Coach looked at him and there was a stillness on the field. For the rest of practice Norval didn't make a sound— but believe me, he was in some kind of pain. He didn't miss a practice, and he played in the next game.[2]

*Youngest brother **Joe Lombardi** offered this summary of his
brother's coaching style at Saints:*

He had a couple of assistant coaches, but he did everything.
He delegated things, but he had a watchful eye for everything
out there. He spent time with his ballplayers; very hands-on.
Everything in practice was repeated constantly. He felt that
every play should be a touchdown. And it's true, if every play
is executed correctly. We had a modified T-formation offense
with one back behind the quarterback. He was using the
Notre Dame offense and modified it just a bit. We also ran
the sweep, which he carried all the way through his pro
career. That was a great play and for some reason it always
worked. I pulled on that play, but then the guards pulled on
almost every play. Even if it was a short play, we'd take a step
back after the snap and hit the defensive players as they came
in. During scrimmages, he would always position himself in
the offense, behind the backfield. You could watch everything from there—you could see your offense unfold the play
and could get a good eye of the defense.

We were in great shape in high school, no question
about it, and he was a great motivator. He prided himself on
that all the way through his career, and the same was true
with calisthenics and running. We always had a few laps
around the field and we always had a lot of sprints. And if
you did something wrong, you did a lot of laps. But that was
pretty normal for most coaches.

He didn't live too far from us, but we never talked that
much. He had his own family. I was a ballplayer for him and
that was it. I saw more of Marie than I saw of him. Marie, my

wife, Betty, and I became close, but there was always that distance between Vince and me. My last memories of Vince: I really don't have any. Even when we had family reunions, he wasn't there. He was busy, away at a Super Bowl, or doing something else.

Lombardi was tough on the football field, and he could be just as much an ogre in the classroom. But the bluster didn't hide the fact that Lombardi also was a crack teacher. **Larry Higgins:**

I had Lombardi for both physics and chemistry. I had come to Saints before my junior year, along with another guy by the name of Dave Finley. Talk about a kid advanced for his years. I mean, Finley was already built like a pro football player. He had muscles from his toes to the top of his head, and he was one of my best friends. On our first day of practice, you know, with us as the brand-new kids, Finley was throwing around other linemen out there like they were ragdolls. You had to see it to believe it, and it was obvious that he was going to make a big impression on the team.

Dave was also kind of a wise guy, and it showed up in the classroom. Anyway, there wasn't a seat for him in chemistry class, so he had to sit at a desk that was actually behind Lombardi. Lombardi would be teaching and behind him was this one desk and Finley was there. At one point Finley fell asleep. Some girls started snickering and Lombardi turned around, livid when he saw Dave there with his head on his desk. Even though this guy was going to be a big asset to his football team, Lombardi said, "You are out of here, and you are off the team." After that, Dave left school and joined the navy.

Another time in school, I was going along in second-year algebra, which was absolute Greek to me. I didn't know what the heck was going on. A Mrs. Keegan was a very devoted, devout teacher, but she just wasn't getting this stuff into my head. One day Mrs. Keegan was sick. The head sister came into our classroom and told us that because Mrs. Keegan was sick, Mr. Lombardi would take over. I thought, *My God, I've got him in chemistry and physics and now in algebra.* So he came in and started teaching algebra and, amazing thing, all of a sudden I started to understand it. It turned out that Mrs. Keegan was sick that whole week, so we had Lombardi for algebra the entire week and no longer was Mrs. Keegan speaking Greek to me after she came back. Lombardi had an incredible ability to teach almost anything, doing so in a way that was easy to understand.

When you were a ballplayer taking one of Lombardi's classes, you knew he was going to call on you. He liked to make an example out of the athletes, so you had to study. Years later, I was taking a chemistry class at Fordham, and by this time guys were getting drafted to go fight in the Korean War. There was pressure to do well in your courses because otherwise the draft board would be coming after you. One of the electives I had to take was chemistry. As it turns out, I did really well in the course. That was because of what Lombardi had taught me years before. He really was quite a teacher.

I think what made him so good was his dedication. He'd go down the aisles and he'd be teaching with a very strong voice that couldn't be tuned out. But you got the impression that he was genuinely interested in what he was teaching, so you said to yourself that this was something you needed to be interested in, too. And it was the same way in football. You could see the things that he was teaching were working, and so you were hanging on every word he said because you knew damn well that it would benefit you as a ballplayer. And it was that same way, with the same atmosphere and the same feeling, in the classroom. He was a great coach, but I think he was an even better teacher.

Higgins recalls one of his most memorable games at Saints:

It was also one of our worst. It was an annual game in which the best team in Bergen County and the best team in Hudson County would play each other in what they called the Union Bowl Game. In my junior year, when I was hardly playing, we were playing Lincoln and it was 0 to 0 late in the game. Vince finally told me to go in. I went in and scored on a touchdown run of about twenty or thirty yards. That made it 6-0, and that's how the game ended.

The next year, our opponent in the game was Union Hill, the best team in Hudson County. We really had a very fine team, but we got overconfident. Earlier in the year, we had beaten by about forty points a team that in turn had beaten Union Hill. And Lombardi just couldn't bring us to the point where we were not overconfident.

It was a very, very cold day in early November, and the ground was as hard as cement. We would have been okay if we had been in sneakers, but we wore our cleats. That whole day was a miserable day. Nothing we did worked, and everything they did worked. But it was 0-0 and that's the way the game ended, 0-0. Nobody scored. But this is where I learned that Lombardi had terrible eyesight. At one point in the ball game, we got down to what could not have been more than twenty yards from the goal line. It was like third down when Lombardi sent in a running play. In the huddle, I said, "No, no, no. Let me try to kick a field goal. We're right in front of the goalpost!" And Billy White, our quarterback, said, "No, no, the coach said to run the ball."

So I broke out of the huddle, looked over toward Lombardi, and gave him a kicking motion, suggesting that we go for the field goal. He didn't see it; his eyesight was so poor. He must have later gotten some kind of operation because his eyes were better later on in life. But he couldn't see me, because after the game was over I said, "Coach, you know we should have kicked a field goal." And he said, "That's right, we should have. Why didn't you let me know?" I said, "Coach, I broke away from the huddle and was out in the middle of the field giving the sign for kicking." He said, "I didn't see it."

DeGasperis knew that Lombardi was tough as nails, but that the coach also had a big heart and had few peers as an inspirational leader:

I played guard and linebacker for him in 1943, when I was a freshman, and after the season I was accidentally shot by a friend of mine with a .22-caliber bullet. I spent eighteen days in the hospital, and every doctor told me my playing days were over. Father Tim [Moore] and the coach visited me several times. Coach Lombardi told me the doctors said I wouldn't be playing any more football but that they were wrong. He said I'd be in uniform the next year. The bullet was never removed, and I played football not only in high school but also in prep school. In 1951 I captained the University of Delaware team.[3]

One of Lombardi's former players at Saints, who requests anonymity, tells an interesting story about how his coach was able to get his hands on a valuable commodity that was a great teaching aid for Lombardi:

My [relative] played football for Notre Dame under Frank Leahy, and during his junior year he came home from school with the Notre Dame playbook so he could study it. I grabbed it and brought it to Lombardi for him to take a look at. Now that was in the days when we didn't have photocopiers, just that blue mimeograph paper that would smudge your hands.

So a school administrator, a secretary, myself, and Lombardi started cranking it out, duplicating every single thing that was in that playbook. My [relative] went to his death never knowing I had done this. I certainly never told him. We duplicated Frank Leahy's T right down to the last word, and I was able to return it before my [relative] even knew that I had taken it. When Lombardi first saw that playbook, it was like he was looking at the Holy Grail. He went nuts when I presented it to him.

Joe Lombardi, *fifteen years Vince's junior, hadn't really been cognizant of who his brother was until Vince was off at Fordham:*

14

I can remember back to when he was a player at Fordham and his coming back home, sometimes with his friends, to have dinner with us. He was always the big brother, although I wasn't close to him. He was gone most of the time, and he was fifteen years older than me. I kind of idolized him. That's the way I was as a young boy. There never was a comparison made by my parents between sons in the sense of one outdoing the other. He was my best man at my wedding in 1951; that was the older brother in him. But we never had a conversation about that at all.

Larry Higgins *recalls his senior year at Saints and winning a state championship with Lombardi:*

It was really a great effort by the entire team. Lombardi was determined to be very successful and we *were* very successful. We were a very, very honed team all because of Lombardi. It was actually a disadvantage to the other schools because Lombardi had us playing like college freshmen or college seniors. We just rolled over everyone.

At one point during his eight-year stay at Saints, Lombardi got a sweet job offer from a rival high school, and it appeared he was all set to go. **Higgins** *remembers:*

Lombardi was revered as a saint. But he was only making about seven hundred dollars a year or something like that, and that included his teaching chemistry and physics. And he was

15

a substitute teacher, too, who could walk in and teach any subject at all, and I can testify to that. But anyway, he was actually revered by the whole school, as well he should be. The rumors of his leaving were in the local newspaper. I told him once that deep down in my heart I felt that he should make the move. "Take the job," I said. "You deserve it. Get the hell out of this place, because all we're playing for here are medals and holy pictures." All the nuns had apparently heard the rumors, too, because one day they gathered together all the kids in the schoolyard and then went and got Lombardi. When he came out, everyone started cheering him and yelling for him not to leave. "Oh, Mr. Lombardi, please don't leave!" they shouted over and over. And you know what? He turned that other job down.

*Lombardi eventually did leave Saints, that move coming when he returned to Fordham before the 1947 season to begin a stint that some expected would lead to his taking over the head-coaching position from Ed Danowski. But that never happened. Lombardi's two-year stopover there added seasoning to his coaching experience, but it had to be a downer for someone who had been somewhat of a star at Fordham years earlier as a member of the fabled Seven Blocks of Granite. Good friend and Rams teammate **Jim Lawlor** recalls those earlier years as students at the city school:*

He was quite sensitive about being Italian. We went to a sorority dance once and the minute we got in there he could feel the resentment. They had the dance in the main ballroom of this place, and you came up the stairs through a foyer into the ballroom. We had gone to the men's room and

Lombardi takes an offensive lineman's traditional three-point stance as a member of the 1935 Fordham University football team. As a guard, he was a member of Fordham's fabled Seven Blocks of Granite.

he was about two steps in front of me, and there were five brothers standing by the door and one of them said, "Who's the little Guinea?" and I don't think he even broke stride. He just turned around and let it fly, and this guy's teeth disappeared down his throat and the other four brothers jumped in and I jumped in. We had about five minutes of fun and frolic up on the foyer. I told Vince, "We better get out of here." He said, "You're damn right we better," and we grabbed our coats and we were going down the main stairway when two cops were coming up. They said, "Where's the fight, fellows?" and Vince said, "Right up there," and the two of us took off out the door.[4]

*After Lombardi and Higgins had moved on to Fordham as coach and player, respectively, there was that issue of whether or not Lombardi would eventually replace Danowski as head coach. It never happened as Lombardi stayed there only two years before moving on to West Point, but **Larry Higgins** remembers there being a division of opinion regarding Lombardi's imminent future at Fordham:*

Danowski was popular and Lombardi always respected him as the head coach. But I think Lombardi had been promised something by the Jesuits in coming to Fordham. On the other hand, the New York media loved Danowski, and I think what they said and wrote swayed the school president into keeping Danowski in charge. The writers kept saying, "Who is this unknown that's all of a sudden coming in just when the Fordham team is coming into maturity?" Well, the reason Fordham was coming into maturity was because of Lombardi.

Lombardi used to do all the chalk talk on Mondays; the X's and the O's. One day he was late and Danowski said, "Okay, I'm going up there and fill in for him." Well, he starts putting X's and O's onto the board, and he ended up putting too many X's on one side of the ball—he had twelve guys there. So every time he diagrammed another play, that extra X was still there. All of us players were sitting there watching this, wondering if we should say something, when suddenly Lombardi arrives, soaking wet because he had just come through the rain to get there. He was looking at Danowski's X's and O's, too, and finally got so impatient with it that he says, "Let me do it," and he steps up to the blackboard, erases it and puts eleven on each side. It was really embarrassing for Danowski, but it was also typical of the atmosphere that was there.

Other books and other authors have said that there was a vote taken by the players about who should be head coach and that Danowski had won, but I say that's an absolute lie. There never was a vote of the team. I've been back for reunions and things like that, and I checked this with other ballplayers. What is true, I believe, is that they had promised the job to Lombardi but the judgments were swayed by the press. That was terribly unfair to everybody and it caused a lot of great dissension because, let's face it, the New Jersey guys who Lombardi recruited had come to play for him.

It ended up being a blessing in disguise because who knows where his career track would have taken him had he stayed a number of more years at Fordham as head coach. So things did work out for him.

*Before the Fordham–West Point game in 1949, Fordham players received mysterious post cards with a West Point postmark addressed specifically to them, obviously intended to psyche out the Rams players. **Higgins** got one from his playing counterpart at West Point:*

It said, "I'm going to get you on the field. Your weak ankles, I'm going to break both of them." And this was strange because I really did at one time have weak ankles that gave me problems, although I had since built them up while going to army paratrooper school. But how could this guy have known it? Then I realized—it was Lombardi, and that really disappointed me, that Lombardi, now at West Point, would even give away such information as a psychological ploy.

I told a newspaper interviewer about this and it made it into the paper that I was very disappointed in what Mr. Lombardi had done. Lombardi read it and after Army had ended up beating us pretty badly, 35-0, I think, I was out on the bus getting ready to go back to an inn where the team would change, when Lombardi came onto the bus, came over to me, and put his head right next to mine just like old times, and said, "Larry, I did not give them that information. I don't even know where they got that information, but I would never betray you," and he left the bus. I still don't know where they got the information.

Herbert Seidell, a center who played at Fordham from 1947 through 1949, thinks Lombardi's subsequent West Point experience not only deepened Lombardi's football knowledge, it even toned down his act a bit:

I would say he was volatile when he went to West Point but then got kind of polished up in terms of relating to his peers. I think with Red Blaik you had no choice but to conform. Blaik was a gentleman when you came right down to it.

When Seidell tuned in to watch Lombardi's Packers in the sixties and read about the coach, he surmised that there was a side to Lombardi not often explored:

There was a certain intrigue in watching him have that success knowing that I had been under this same guy fifteen or twenty years earlier. But I have another thought, too. Several times I got the feeling that he recognized his relative position, his fame, although I don't mean to make that sound like an ego thing.

There was one time when I took my son Jimmy to meet Lombardi at some function. Jimmy had been a high school football player, and I had no other aspirations in taking him to meet Lombardi than it might be a good building block for life for him. Vinny was marginally cordial, at best.

Lombardi stayed only two seasons at Fordham, where he fell out of sorts with popular head coach Ed Danowski over a clash of coaching styles. But in leaving Fordham after the 1948 season, Lombardi headed to West Point, where a confluence of coaching greatness was set in motion. Army's head coach still was the legendary Col. **Earl "Red" Blaik**—*who was in need of a new offensive assistant when the eventually legendary Sid Gillman left West Point to take the head-coaching position at the University of Cincinnati. Blaik, who had known practically nothing about Lombardi, was impressed long before he had completed his round of three interviews with the upstart Lombardi:*

I knew he was ready. I saw the sparkle in his eyes. Right then as a young fellow, he had that special quality of being able to electrify a room.[5]

Seidell, *all things considered, believes Lombardi could have been a superb chief executive of a corporation, big or small:*

21

His orderly mind and analytical abilities meant he could really focus on a given business. He could have run any kind of a business that you'd put him in front of. He was a master of detail, but he also knew when to get off the details and to get back to the matter of the total ball game. Even with all the intricacies, it was a matter of people executing a fairly simple system: Get the basic pattern down and then you could build the nuances into that system.

There were just so many things he taught us to do. One was what was called "the cheater step," whereby the back in a split T, who normally sets up three and a half yards behind the ball, would move up a half step closer without being detected by the defense—anything that would get him to the line of scrimmage faster and force the quarterback to hand off the ball more rapidly; in other words, hit the thing as fast as you could. It was all in the details, studied laboriously, such as when to use a crossover step or lead with a different foot. Timing made all the difference. One threat was the quarterback making the first step after getting the ball from center and just driving right back at the hole with a sneak. At times, that can be the best-executed play in the book. But the basics of the system were relatively simple.

Seidell's favorite anecdote about Lombardi concerns the time when serendipitous timing allowed Lombardi to meet Seidell's future mother-in-law in a nice homey setting:

I had just gotten engaged to my wife-to-be Marguerite, and went to New York in December [1951] to meet her mother and make arrangements for our wedding to be held the next year. It turns out that Marguerite's mom lived in an apartment in the Bronx. Anyhow, it ends up that the person living in the next apartment over was Marge Planitz, who I knew was Vinny's sister-in-law. Small world, right?

Well, the last thing I expected to have happen was for my sister-in-law Rose to go next door and who do you suppose they dragged back to the apartment? Vince, who was down visiting, from West Point I suppose, during the holidays. Vince was marvelous. He came over, walked in, and sat down on the piano stool and started telling the story about how I had gotten my face splattered when we had played West Point the year he had gone there to work for Blaik.

What had happened is that I had gotten knocked on my butt after centering the ball for a punt. It was a muddy field and I had gotten clobbered in the face pretty good. The next day the *Daily News* comes out with a story about the game and the photo they run is of me coming off the field with all this gauze hanging off my face. I looked like a friggin' wreck.

So he sits down and tells the whole story about what happened to me—and I get choked up just talking about it. First, he looks at me—and we hadn't seen each other since that game two years earlier—and he says, "Looks like your mouth finally healed up. Did you ever get the tooth replaced?" He certainly had a sense of humor. It may not have been the sharpest, but at least he was trying desperately to be funny. It had been a game in which there had been something like seventeen teeth knocked out of nine mouths. It was one of the games used as evidence when the NCAA was thinking about making face guards mandatory. Somebody said to Vince, "That must have been quite a game," and Vince said, "Yeah, it sure was." Then he turned to my mother-in-law-to-be and said, "In that game, we knew if we got to [quarterback Dick]

Doheny, we would have Fordham's offense in our hands; and if we got to Seidell, we knew we had their spirit." I still get the same lump in my throat telling the story today. That's the best damn compliment I ever received. I cherish that more than if he had said that I had been the best center he ever coached, and he couldn't have said it at a more appropriate time— directed toward people that I was desperately concerned about liking me—my prospective in-laws.

Gene Ward *of the* New York Daily News *described Lombardi by analyzing one of the many speeches he gave to groups:*

There is no more famous football man anywhere, and his ideas are applicable to all the people and all the problems of this trouble-wracked world. He cuts to the heart of things that twist humans and nations. He deals in proven basics. He does not appeal, he challenges and in such a way that his challenge flays your guilt and prods your intellect.[6]

2

WEST POINT

It was at West Point that Lombardi found his true calling. And a home; finally, a place where he could bark orders and instructions to attentive players and still blend into the scenery. Budding Lombardi-types were everywhere, disguised as faculty instructors, tactical officers, and upper-class cadets whose daily mission was, and is, to take wet-behind-the-ears plebes and turn them into crack military leaders sound of mind, strong of heart, fit of body, and thick of skin.

Still, Lombardi had rough edges and he needed someone to help smooth them off. That sculptor was Col. Earl "Red" Blaik, Army's esteemed head coach and the one person who could trump Lombardi when it came to commanding rapt attention upon entering a room or stepping onto a football field. In going to West Point in 1949, Lombardi was stepping into a tradition steeped in American military history and collegiate football excellence. Blaik, a

1920 West Point graduate, served as an Army assistant for seven seasons, through 1933, and returned to the school as head coach after guiding Dartmouth's football program from 1933 through 1940. Between 1944 and 1950, Blaik's West Point teams amassed an incredible 57-3-4 record that included five undefeated seasons, two national titles, and the 1944–46 teams that featured Felix "Doc" Blanchard and Glenn Davis, "Mr. Inside and Mr. Outside," respectively. Lombardi was a nice fit, having himself been a part of collegiate football lore as a member of Fordham's famed Seven Blocks of Granite.

Blaik was probably one of a handful of men in America who had the kind of wisdom and commanding presence needed to harness a colt like Lombardi. Yet the colonel gave the respectful Vince enough rope to be his own man, his own coach, a motivational mastermind who understood all the intricacies involved in playing every position on the field. Someone who not only could explain and diagram football plays all the way from the general X's and O's down to the details of an interior lineman's footwork while pulling on a sweep or the split-second timing of the snap exchange between center and quarterback and the subsequent spin-move handoff to an accelerating fullback hitting the gap on a belly play.

Lombardi joined fast company at West Point, because West Point assistants under Blaik comprised a Who's Who of future college head coaches, men such as Murray War-math (who went on to be a head coach at Mississippi State), John Green (Vanderbilt), Bill Yeoman (Houston), Sid Gill-man (Cincinnati, and later many years in the NFL), Paul Dietzel (Louisiana State University), Herman Hickman (Yale), and Paul Amen (Wake Forest). Granted, Lombardi doesn't make the list because of the technicality that he never actually was a college head coach, but that's a minor point. Consider what he would accomplish with the Green Bay Packers and was apparently getting started with the Redskins before he passed away. Even as a West Point assistant, Lombardi was somebody special, and those who were there at the time (1949–53) remember him as such.

The strict and disciplined leadership environment at West Point was a perfect fit for Lombardi, the ideal training ground for him to harness his own innate abilities and apply them to the football field in ways that would shape him for years to come. **Bill Yeoman** *was there and was also a part of it, and he explains what it was about West Point that fostered a good home for Lombardi and other coaches like him:*

The leadership there would stay up late at night just to devise ways to make things disagreeable for the cadets, and they were very good at it. The thing I have desperately appreciated ever since I left there was what they did to me in terms of teaching me how to be focused to the point where the little knickknacks on the periphery didn't really bother me. As a result of that, you had a good chance of getting done whatever it is you're trying to get done because you don't get caught up in the garbage. I honestly believe if I hadn't gone there, I would have had a tough time.

You got to where you could assess a situation pretty decently, pretty realistically. They spent hours and hours telling you how leaders are supposed to act and explaining to you that the best leader is the one who leads by example. We had leadership lectures, leadership meetings all the time. As a result of that, you got a fairly good idea what was expected of you if you were in a position of responsibility.

When my class showed up there as plebes, we had something like 1,200 kids. It then shrank down to about 800 real quickly. They filled it back up to about 1,050, and then it went down quickly, again, to about 900. We ended up graduating something like 600. And what was so great was that they didn't worry about it if you didn't want to be there. If that was the case, that was your business. Quit and go, and they did very little in trying to talk you into staying. They came to the realization that if they were going to get done what they wanted to get done with a person, he had to want to be there.

Mental toughness is what you're looking for, and you get great help from every part of that place in terms of mental toughness. In the classroom, in drill, everywhere. What's so good about it is that you are graded there every time you turn around, and you are compared every time you turn around. And there's nothing wrong with that, although I'm sure now there are some shrinks who could tell me that it would inhibit somebody, but at the time it was a super deal. So many things now are about being [politically correct], but unfortunately bullets still kill you as easily as they could have back then.

$$\mathcal{J}\!\mathcal{R}$$

Al Paulekas, an offensive lineman under Lombardi at the academy, remembers well the regimentation that pervaded West Point and Army football, as well as a special visitor who would sometimes join the team for trips out of town:

When we traveled, everything was scheduled right to the minute. Practice, when you formed up, when the buses arrived. Everywhere we went there were police escorts for our buses. The first seat on the right was Colonel Blaik's seat, and, typically, Vince would sit with Colonel Blaik. There were two exceptions to that, and one was General MacArthur, in which case Vince would sit in the second seat. That's because MacArthur was Blaik's hero. If you read the books about Blaik, you will see many, many references to his personal contacts with MacArthur during the glory days during the war and during the period after the scandal [the West Point academic-cheating scandal of 1951, in which many cadets were dismissed from the academy, including a number of football players, among them Blaik's quarterback son, Robert]. Vince knew his place.

We always stayed at nice places when we traveled. The Army-Penn game was a big game for us, played two weeks before the Navy game. We would always play in Franklin Field, and we always stayed at the Merchants & Manufacturers Country Club. The morning of the game, Vince was up early and the guys would take a walk. Some would take the walk with Vince and some would take a walk with Colonel Blaik. And the ones that took a walk with Vince were the Catholic boys, because Vince took us to Mass and walked with us. And as tough as he was, he was a very religious guy, a very pious man. And that wasn't the least bit phony. That was a major facet of his life. He could be the toughest, most miserable bastard you ever played for, yet the most gentle guy in the world.

APWIDE WORLD PHOTOS

Lombardi keeps a watchful eye over a drill featuring quarterbacks and centers at West Point. He had his work cut out for him: This is August 29, less than two months after the football team had been decimated by an academic scandal that resulted in about forty players being kicked out of the academy.

Paulekas *addresses the Blaik-Lombardi connection:*

Colonel Blaik set the policy and was up on some kind of a pedestal. In fact, his desk was one step above the office floor. The messages that Blaik conveyed, Vince conveyed. But Vince could sit on the bench and in the sweaty locker room and tell you the same thing in a way that was more on your level. He was more of a people person. Blaik was the master technician, our leader, our general—he was our five-star general. Vince, on the other hand, was the colonel you could talk to. And Colonel Blaik never called anybody by their first name; he called you by your last name. With Vince, some-times I was Paulekas, but a lot of times I was Al. Vince left my senior year, unfortunately for me. In fact, when he left, the other guys said, "He'll never make it in pro ball, because who is going to take his [crap]?"

West Point had been the perfect fit for him. Had Vince not come to West Point and had Vince not met Colonel Blaik, I think he still would have been a successful coach because he had all the skills and talents. What he got from Blaik were the real refinements, all those little holes that filled the dike. And he had players who would do whatever was demanded of them. You don't get that anywhere else.

One thing that Vince used to get a big kick out of, and Blaik would turn his head, was when fights would break out in practice. Scrimmages could get rather intense, particularly in spring training. And Vince and Doc [Blanchard] were always very slow to break up the fight. Vince would sit there and laugh like hell watching two guys trying to kill each other. And then they'd stop it and calm everybody down, and by the time you got back to the dressing room, everybody was friends again.

It was tough all around. One time I got my mouth cut open pretty badly in practice, and I had to get about twenty stitches—but only after practice was over. And I didn't miss practice the next day. In those days, you know, we didn't wear face guards.

Cleveland native **Jerry Lodge** *had offers to play football from a lot of schools such as Ohio State, Princeton, Michigan, and Cincinnati, but he chose West Point. That's where he had wanted*

to go since he was in fourth grade, and it turned out to be a good move because that's how he was able to meet and play for Red Blaik and, of course, Vince Lombardi. He arrived there in 1950:

I had played fullback among other positions in high school, but one month into my first season at West Point, they decided I was going to be an offensive guard. I don't think West Point had had a guard in the previous ten years, or at least as long as Blaik had been there, who hadn't played fullback. You had to be fast enough to lead and to be able to pull out and lead around the ends, and that means you've got to be as fast as the backs. So that's why I was made an offensive guard.

During my junior year they needed help at linebacker, so I was moved to there. As a matter of fact I was the linebacker who called defensive signals. While I didn't have much contact with Lombardi during the week, I did during games because he always sat upstairs, where he was on the phones with Blaik watching what was going on both offensively and defensively. As the defensive signal caller, that meant I would get on the headphones with him when I came to the sideline, and he would tell me what he thought we ought to call and why and what changes we ought to make and other things.

What was truly amazing to me was how Lombardi was able to watch and take in so much going on all over the field. I don't know how many football games you watch or how seriously you watch them or try to discern certain things, but it's really hard to sit there and watch a football game and figure out what more than one or two players are doing at any given time. Stuff just happens so fast. Yet Lombardi somehow was always able to do that and able to tell me what people were doing. One after the other he would tell me what each of our guys was doing right or wrong and what their guys were doing right or wrong, or what was different from what we had thought they were going to do. And then we would have all these assignment changes or alignment changes or whatever he felt we ought to do. And I was always extremely impressed with his really unusual ability to discern all that. There's no doubt in my mind that Lombardi had to be some sort of incredible intellectual. One of the things I concluded in my short career as an athlete was that there is a vast difference between someone who knows what the hell he is doing and someone who doesn't. For example, in high school we had a blocking rule in which the right guard pulls out and goes around the right end and leads the back down the field. That's it. Well, that's not the Lombardi rule. The Lombardi rule was that the right guard splits his stance a little bit more than normal, a half a foot maybe, and upon the snap he lowers his right shoulder and pulls his left leg across the front of his body toward the backfield. Then he crosses over with his right foot and starts to run around the end by bowing around the end. As he gets near the point where he's going to go up field, he dips his left shoulder and begins to pivot around as he runs, running in a low crouch, head up, looking around for tacklers. The idea is to have a little bit of a hook to your run so that you are actually looking inside rather than up the field.

The whole thing on offense was choreographed. Every single play. We would practice pulling out and we would practice cross-blocking until we were blue in the face, where every single movement was choreographed exactly the way he wanted it. He had all this broken down, this step, next step, next step, next step. And that's the way he practiced, one, two, three, four. And if you didn't get the exact right position, he would make you do it again until you finally figured out that you had to do it exactly right. You couldn't just kind of slop it around. And he would demonstrate a lot of this himself. Lombardi was unusual in the respect that he could, in essence, envision the way everything should be done and then communicate it so well.

Lodge remembers not only the octave level of Lombardi's yelling voice but the distinct pitch as well:

He was a very emotional guy. He had kind of a high-pitched, squeally voice, so it was kind of funny. We used to kid around, particularly behind his back. It was funny.

*As much as Lombardi yelled on the field, he was all business on the headphones as **Lodge** can attest to:*

He didn't try to cram down too much stuff at once. He was very forward, and every now and then he would get a little upset if somebody made a mistake and we got hurt. But other than that, no ranting and raving.

There was a strict code of conduct at West Point, which probably could have been written up just as well by Lombardi. It was a demanding code of conduct, one that Lombardi respected and

one he understood he didn't need to take up another notch on his own. **Lodge** *explains:*

Lombardi had a lot of respect for the fact that players had a lot on their minds besides football. And I think he always stopped short of really punishing the guys for things because he realized that their life was tough enough without him adding to it. That didn't mean that he wouldn't get in your face sometimes.

Another thing is that he was always the coach who supervised the end of practice, and there was this fetish at West Point about conditioning. It was unbelievable how much better conditioned we were than any team that we played. That was based in part on the demands of both Blaik and Lombardi, and also the fact that it was very hard for anybody to get out of shape at West Point. But at the end of practice, Lombardi had this little technique called a "grass drill," where you would run until he blew the whistle, at which point you would hit the ground. And then he'd blow the whistle and you'd pop up and run forward. And then he would blow the whistle and you would go to the ground. He did that with the Packers, apparently, but if you ever tried it, it was really tiring to do that kind of stuff. And we would do that for only about seven or eight minutes. He would do it for five minutes if he wasn't mad, but if he was mad he would do it for eight minutes or even ten. And that was the only way he would manifest his pleasure with performance.

Peter Vann *was one of the young men who played quarterback at West Point during the Lombardi years there. He was a plebe*

during that fateful summer of '51, when the academic scandal nearly broke the back of Army football:

I entered West Point that summer, and everyone was higher than a kite because of the expectations for the football team that fall. We were allowed to fall out on July 4 and I remember it distinctly because I had entered on July 3. I couldn't understand what was happening, because everyone was running around like ants on a hill, with people in civilian suits all around the place. Effectively, the investigation had broken open just then, and, consequently, a whole bunch of guys got asked to leave, including quarterback Bobby Blaik, the coach's son, and many, many others, to include thirty-eight football players. But we continued playing the same schedule that year, to include playing against Frank Gifford who was at Southern California. I think we won two games that year.

If you draw a graph, a curve, of Lombardi's career, it would look like a sine curve. He would be up higher than high with that flashing smile with the gap between the teeth and he could get down lower than low. He was very emotional, going from an emotional high to an emotional low. Before that curbing scandal, he had been on an emotional high the previous two years because things were going very well for Vince and he wasn't a spring chicken. Because of the scandal, Lombardi and Blaik both damn near quit football. Lombardi was so devastated he went back to Fordham to get counsel. He got counsel from Blaik and counsel from anyone who would sit and listen to him.

The next year we won six and lost four, and we beat some teams that we weren't supposed to beat. The year after that, we lost our first game, but won all the rest, making people ask, "Where did these guys come from?" We weren't supposed to win, but we beat Duke, we beat Michigan with Ron Kramer, and we beat Tulane.

David Maraniss, *writing about Lombardi's first week on the job at West Point in 1949, when he and fellow first-year assistant coach Murray Warmath had to spend several hours a day at the blackboard diagramming and explaining formations and plays with Col. Red Blaik grilling them all the while:*

It was a variation of Lombardi's first job interview, but this time for keeps. At one point Lombardi found himself in a heated debate with Blaik and the other assistants over the proper way to deliver the center's snap to the quarterback. Blaik had always taught the half-turn of the ball, presenting it to the quarterback sideways. Lombardi preferred the quarter-turn, with the ball reaching the quarterback at a slight angle. It was quicker, he said, and made it easier for the quarterback to hand off or pass. Blaik disagreed, so they got out a ball and practiced both methods there in the conference room outside Blaik's office. The quarter-turn proved faster by a fraction of a second.[1]

Sid Gillman *long has been considered one of the true master-minds of the passing offense. Among his other contributions to the game, he says, was his role in helping Lombardi get a job pro-motion—twice:*

As a matter of fact, I brought Vince in to coach at West Point. I was the line coach for Red Blaik at West Point at the time.

I'd replaced Herman Hickman, who went on to Yale. One day Blaik pulled me aside. He said I needed an assistant. He'd invited this guy in and wanted me to interview him. If I wanted him there, we'd hire him. He said the fellow had been coaching at a small Catholic high school in Brooklyn [actually, Englewood, New Jersey]. So Vince came over for a couple of days and we became friends. Then I left to go to the University of Cincinnati and they hired Vince, but not to take my place. He was an extra coach. Murray Warmath replaced me and he was actually the one who hired Vince. . . .

Then early in 1959, we were at a league meeting in Philadelphia. I went into the men's room and there was a guy there I hadn't seen since I was in college at Ohio State and working at a department store in Columbus. I was shocked to see this guy there in Philadelphia. We'd been friends in school, and I asked him what he was doing. He said he had his own department store in Green Bay and he was looking for a coach. He was the chairman of the selection committee to find a coach for the Packers. I asked him if he'd be interested in Vince and he said he would be.

So I went back out and found Vince. I said, "Vince, there's a buddy of mine out here looking for a coach for Green Bay. Would you be interested?" He said yes he would. I said, "I'll talk to him and make arrangements for you two to get together." Now, I don't know that that's what got the job for Vince, but I think I played a part in his getting it.[2]

As much as the power sweep became identified with Lombardi and the Packers in the sixties, there never really was a question that it was a play that had pre-Lombardi roots. **Sid Gillman** *explains:*

Lombardi's signature play was the power sweep. I used a quick toss. To a lot of people, they looked the same. In fact, Red Hickey, who coached the San Francisco 49ers, said the first time he saw the Lombardi sweep was when I ran it with the Rams. There was a difference, though. Lombardi ran an option sweep; ours was predicated on getting outside.

What Lombardi did was set up an option based on the tight end's block. As the halfback came across for the ball, he didn't run at full speed. He came with controlled speed so that he could key the block of the tight end on the linebacker. If the tight end took him out, the ball carrier broke inside. If he took him in, the ball carrier broke outside. Paul Hornung was made to order for that kind of sweep. He wasn't a speedster. He had good speed but not intense speed. With Lombardi's sweep, because of the option aspect, the line was loosened up a little bit. It was inside-outside on the block for his tight end.[3]

*Lineman **Bruce Elmblad**'s stay at West Point allowed him to play under Sid Gillman and then Vince Lombardi, a pair of offense-oriented coaches with a divergence of personal styles:*

Sid Gillman would be the entrepreneur and Lombardi the CEO. That is, Lombardi was more the operating kind, nuts and bolts. The thing about Red Blaik is that he was a no-nonsense guy with a knack for bringing in great assistant coaches who had bright minds. When you worked for Colonel Blaik, you were going someplace.

One of Lombardi's quarterbacks at West Point was **Gil Reich,** *who had come out of high school as a single-wing tail-back before Coaches Blaik and Lombardi turned him into a T-formation quarterback:*

One of the things I recall with Coach Lombardi is that he spent a great deal of time working on my footwork. There was a lot of intricate footwork required of a T quarterback, things like pivoting for a handoff or drops for a pass. And I think they saw in me a good prospect for that because I had also been a successful defensive back in high school back in Pennsylvania.

I played my plebe [freshman] year as a starter, then I was backup the next year to Coach Blaik's son, Robert, at quarterback. I was a starter on defense at safety at the same time. During that time, we had a close relationship with our backfield coach, that is, Coach Lombardi. He was a tough, demanding perfectionist. His idea of practice was running the same play over and over and over and over until we all got it right. Practice makes perfect.

The other thing I recall in conjunction with Lombardi and West Point was the introduction of what we called audibles. We'd call the play at the huddle, come to the line of scrimmage, and in a few seconds the quarterback would look over and read the defense, so to speak, and if necessary adjust the play at the line of scrimmage with some verbal changes. Audibles are pretty common nowadays, but that was a whole new twist back then. That was my first introduction to that, and that was important to our offense. Coach Lombardi also insisted that the quarterbacks not only know their own positions on every play and their own signals, but everyone else's assignment on every play as well. Like I said, he was very demanding.

Now, I had been a tailback in high school in the single-wing offense, so I had called the plays there in the huddle but never had had to call audibles. And I had also had to have some knowledge of other assignments when I was playing high school ball, but we didn't go into anywhere near the depth in high school that we would with Lombardi at West Point with the T-formation and the audible system.

The demands that Coach Lombardi put on us served me well when I got to Kansas because I was light-years ahead of my competitors there for the quarterback position. I think maybe a few bigtime schools were doing those same things we had been doing at West Point, such as the audibles. I knew only that we were one of the leading programs at that time in doing things like that.

As an offensive-minded coach first and foremost, Lombardi considered it his duty to pour as much of his brain matter as he could into the heads of young quarterbacks, who, like **Reich,** *learned quickly that it was their duty to put into practice what Lombardi had drilled into them:*

He spent a great deal of time with us watching film, going over game plans and strategies. He spent a lot of time on the fundamentals. He was very strict, very demanding, very precise. There were times that his insistence on perfection caused a lot of frustration. He would push you to the extreme. I remember some of our fellow backfield people would come into the locker room and were so upset with the pressure that the coach was putting on them, they swore they would pick a fight with him next time it happened. Of course, that never happened.

His instruction with us was very hands-on, and he would demonstrate himself the moves he wanted you to make. Of course, he wasn't as young and athletic as we were at the time, so his demonstration would be more in theory. But he would get behind center and demonstrate what he wanted you to do, and then it was your turn to get there and do it time after time after time. The whole system at West Point was very demanding and very disciplined, but you didn't have the everyday, seasonal close contact with tactical officers that I had with Coach Lombardi. Every afternoon for two hours he was there and he was concentrating. It was up close and personal.

Everything at West Point was about details, consistency, ingraining the right way for doing things, focus, and discipline. Those virtues carried over into Red Blaik's football programs well. Few stones were left unturned and there was a thoroughness to everything done there, with thoroughness and simplicity being key ingredients of what made Army a national power in those days, as **Bill Yeoman** *describes:*

We filmed every practice. We'd go home and have dinner, and then we'd go back to the office and go over the practice film. That's why I was with Vince most every night, and I tell you he doesn't come anywhere near as close to being as good to be with as my wife.

The old man [Blaik] handled the projector, going back and forth, back and forth. What we did was look at every kid; look where he put his steps, look at where he put his head, look for any false moves, look for anything that he did wrong.

Then you'd work on all that stuff the next day, every day. This included all the drills, not just the scrimmages.

We were very conscious of technique because we were not real big; we weren't going to overpower anyone. We were going to have to make sure we finessed them, that we had good leverage with everything we did. Everything had to be done halfway decently. If you've got a philosophy, something you believe in, you can explain it several different ways. If you're just giving a team a play and telling them to go run it and don't know why you're doing it, it makes it more difficult to be as expressive as Vince was in that he knew a number of ways to convey the same information so that it sounded fresh every time. He knew what he was after, and that's not the case with a lot of coaches. They never, ever develop a philosophy. They end up not really *believing in* much of anything. That doesn't mean they don't win games, because they'll get kids who can run plays really well. But it means that many coaches don't fully understand why they are or are not winning.

Because we couldn't overpower anybody, we had better have all the angles figured out. You had to understand precisely what you're after and then transmit that to everyone, and those people have to be receptive to what they are told and receptive to making whatever changes or adjustments were needed to execute those things properly. Not everyone, not even at West Point, had that level of commitment. I'll never forget even if I live to be a thousand that what impressed me as much as anything was the year after Doc Blanchard and Glenn Davis and that bunch left, we did not have that much coming back. We had one kid named Jim Schultz, who was about six-four, 240 pounds, and could literally run the sprints on the track team in addition to holding the All-East records in the hammer throw and the shot. The guy was a friggin' freak. I think he was a tackle.

We played Villanova in the opener that year. We had a tarp around the field and would go through an opening in the tarp to get out onto the field. On the Monday after the Villanova game, we couldn't help but notice when Jim Schultz came through the tarp onto the field, the old man motioned for him to come over, where they stood and talked for a couple of minutes. Then Jim just turned around and walked back off the field, back through the tarp. After some interested looks were exchanged among the rest of the team, the old man called us together and he just said, "Jim is a fine person, a great athlete, but he just doesn't want to play hard enough to be an Army football player." I don't know how all the rest of the players felt, but that surely did inspire me.

Jim was the best athlete we had on the team, but what I'm trying to tell you is that with Colonel Blaik, everything about a football player started in the heart and the head. And if you didn't have that, he didn't care about your body. Schultz's problem was that he didn't play hard enough. He was the biggest guy on the team by far and the best athlete on the team by far. We didn't have very many players, but we still won. We were maybe 5-2-2 in that '47 season, then in '48 we were undefeated again. It's all in the mind.

The athletes now are pretty good kids and magnificent athletes, but if you ever demanded of them now what was demanded of guys thirty or forty years ago, they would be unbelievable as performers if they responded. I say *if*. Unbelievable because they are such great physical specimens. But they would have trouble playing against those old knotheads that we had then, because every time the ball was snapped, they would be getting it right in the mouth. It's a different world now.

West Point was an unbelievable place to coach because you knew the guys weren't out chasing around. You knew they were in their rooms studying, that they were in bed after taps played at ten o'clock, and you knew that they were going to get up at 5:50 in the morning. You knew what they were going to do all day, and they were around people over them doing whatever they could to make themselves disagreeable. It was just so they could tone these guys' minds. It's a superb place. You just had to stay focused on why you were there, and sometimes that meant just gritting your teeth and saying, "If you think you're going to run me off, you're crazy. You haven't seen the day that you can whip me." And you'd have to say that to yourself once in a while.

Lombardi seemed surprisingly small in stature upon meeting him for the first time, especially considering how he had been one of the legendary Seven Blocks of Granite at Fordham. One of the players at West Point, a linebacker and fullback-turned-center, saw Lombardi in his own unique way:

I wouldn't say he was small. He was short, probably not much more than five foot nine, but he was pretty broad shouldered. Chunky, too.

*At West Point and with Lombardi as a coach, players always had to be on the alert to be inserted into a new position on several days' notice, as **Hardy Stone** discovered in 1949:*

I was getting to play a lot in the first two games that season, with the third game to be at Ann Arbor [Michigan] against the Wolverines, who had been national champs the year before. One of our offensive guards got hurt and for reasons unknown to me to this day, they elected not to go with the second-team guard and moved me over there instead. I was called in and told I had to learn a new position.

I would have to go out an hour early to practice, and Jack Green [another Army assistant] and Vince worked with me. I learned how to pull right and how to pull left and all these other tricky things and how to drop back for pass protection and then learn the plays—it was a hell of a deal. It was just, "Up down, up down, again, again, again, again, again. Up down, up down. No, no, no, no." It seems that's all I heard for about an hour.

Having played defense, I didn't know a thing about blocking the sides and that kind of stuff. But I learned it and I played in that game. That put me on the field for the entire game, on both offense and defense. I was so embarrassed about it that every time the defense trotted off the field for the offense to take over, I would trot off with the defense and then trot right back on with the offense. I had to: Otherwise I would have been standing out in the middle of the field in front of ninety-seven thousand people, and I sure as heck didn't want to do that. Oh, yeah; we won the game, 21-7.

Lombardi used many tactics with his offense to keep defenses off-balance, such as constantly changing the rhythm of the quarter-back's signal cadence, or even an unpredictable snap count, as one of his players recalls it:

One time I remember him saying that we would use a three-count in which after the second count we would go as soon as someone coughs in the stands. We were usually a little smaller than the other teams and had to resort to anything we could to get an edge. We beat Michigan my last year and Duke another time and some other good teams—everybody but Navy.

Al Paulekas on one of the lighter moments of playing football at West Point when Lombardi was around:

During spring football after the scandal, we were down in Shea Stadium—the West Point one by the river, not where the Mets play in New York—and we had just had a pretty good workout. Practice was pretty much over and some of the guys were just throwing the ball around, waiting for the bus to come get us and take us back to the locker room. About that time a rep from Voit, the ball maker, shows up.

After the war you couldn't get pigskin because it was at a premium. But Voit was trying to develop a rubber football that would have all the characteristics of the regular pigskin. So the Voit guy came up to show us some test footballs they were trying out. He gave us some of the test balls to play around with, and we started playing a game of kicking field goals and getting off some punts. Soon it was Doc's [Blanchard's] turn to kick, and he kicked the ball one hundred yards. The Voit guy sees this and says, "Uh-oh, I think the rubber is too live." Vince was there, our ol' resident Block of Granite, and *he* starts kicking the ball sixty-five, seventy yards. I'll never forget the expression on that Voit guy's face, or Vince's face for that matter, either.

On Army game day, Lombardi was stationed up in the coaches'
box, linked to the sideline by a telephone headset. Lombardi
wasn't just an omniscient observer from up high—he was pretty
much running the show. Quarterback **Peter Vann** *recalls:*

Blaik was a strategist and he would give the strategy to Lombardi, and Lombardi would have to effectively put the "tacti-
calness" into it—the timing, the looking at defenses and
switching plays, the play-calling sequence, et cetera. Blaik
would call about the first eight plays and then he would kind
of leave it up to his quarterback to call the remaining plays.
Lombardi was never on the bench; he was always upstairs in
the box. The colonel really wasn't a sideline coach. He was a
Monday-to-Friday coach. The first guy I talked to and spent
most of the time with was Lombardi up in that box.

He was yelling at me a lot. And you know after he would
get over his yelling, Vince would really start talking—he
always called me "Pee-TAH" in that New York accent. The
genius of Lombardi is that you don't realize at the time that
you're working with a genius because of all the stuff you're
having to go through. Just like I didn't realize when I had
the camera in my hand that I would someday love to have a
picture of Vince Lombardi and myself. That was just kind of
the naiveté of the kid at the time. He would go with the
strategy of what the next two or three sequences of plays
would be when we got back on the field. And if we fumbled,
I'd really catch the devil when I got back.

One of our most effective set of plays was what we called
our belly series. Out of a straight T backfield, we'd have the
right halfback diving and the fullback coming up right off the

halfback's butt. While the quarterback is putting the ball into the fullback's stomach, he's actually looking to see what the defensive end is doing. If the end is staying or committing upfield, the fullback keeps the ball. If not, the quarterback pulls it back, flips it to the trailing back, and you've got a big gainer going. In the 1953 Navy game, one of our guys scored three touchdowns, two of them off that series. There's a newspaper picture from that game that shows a hole that we could have driven a truck through. Lombardi perfected that with us to a point that it was one of our mainstays. If you look at his playbook at Green Bay, you'd see our playbook. The so-called student body right [sweep plays with lots of blockers]? That was our playbook. Hornung and Taylor; yeah, that was our playbook. Even the pass patterns with [Boyd] Dowler—we had the same thing at West Point.

We played just basic football, and my last two years we were ranked first offensively in the nation.

Even though Lombardi had been a squatty, rock-solid guard at Fordham, he knew enough about quick feet and a quarterback's perspective to teach Vann [and others] plenty of things they might not otherwise have learned. **Vann:**

Lombardi was often a pain in the butt. There was a dive play for me in which I had a sort of flying foot. For some reason, my right foot would come back before it would go up in the line of scrimmage. Our backs were only about three yards back, and we were really popping. It was almost like the hole would open for an instant and then close. That was the type of blocking that was being taught by Blaik. And by my foot coming back, I was losing a crucial fraction of a second. Seeing this in practice, Lombardi would stand behind me with a big forearm over my head looking right at my right foot and as soon as that thing moved a fraction back, I got blasted. Literally, *blasted*.

My third season turned out to be Lombardi's fifth, and last, at West Point. One time Coach Blaik said to everyone, "Bring your cameras out tomorrow and you can get pictures of you and all the coaches or the other players." I brought my camera out and took a picture of every coach and me— that is, every coach except Lombardi. I didn't want the guy's picture because he had just made me work so damn hard. And in looking back at that, I really kick myself. I've got a beautiful picture of Colonel Blaik and myself, but no picture of Lombardi and Peter Vann.

Lombardi, on Red Blaik's calming him down:

He toned down my temper, or tried to. When I'd get too intense and explosive on the field, he'd call me into the office the next day and sit there and look at me and twirl his class ring—West Point 1920—and say, "Vince, we just don't do it that way at West Point. You can't talk that way to cadets. You can't drive them that way because they're being driven all day."[4]

Bill Yeoman *played football at West Point, spent about a year and a half there as an assistant, and later went on to become an*

*assistant at Michigan State under Duffy Daugherty before
moving in 1961 to become the head coach at the University of
Houston, where he remained for about twenty-five years.
Yeoman was another one of Red Blaik's many assistants to
become successful head coaches elsewhere, and he remembers
Lombardi from his days alongside the Hudson River as a real go-
getter who was probably more subservient to Blaik than people
who only knew Lombardi from his NFL days would expect:*

Lombardi had a huge laugh, enjoyed a good time, worked
intensely hard, had great enthusiasm, and was a very committed person. At that time, though, compared to Colonel Blaik,
he was like Mary's little lamb. Colonel Blaik was exceptionally intense. Vince was firm and all that, but I think he got a
little bit of his real seriousness to a certain degree from
Colonel Blaik, because Vince loved to laugh. He didn't have
any problem with that at all. He was stern, but that guy knew
how to tell a joke and knew how to enjoy a joke. He had a
huge ol' belly laugh. I mean, he had a good time.

Colonel Blaik ran the offense, and sometimes we would
change a serious amount of the offense on Thursday afternoon. But no one really got bothered, because when it came
time to play on Saturday, we would just revert back to the
same basic game plan. We were going to run a short trap, a
G block off-tackle, sweep, and throw the pass. Four basic
plays. Whatever we did we could do in our sleep against anything that an opponent put up there against us. There wasn't
anything that we couldn't do, and there wasn't any defense
that we couldn't block. We would just get it right.

We had good quickness without exception, but we
weren't real big. There's no question that all of what I'm
talking about in reference to those Army teams would also

be characteristic of those Green Bay Packers teams of Lombardi's in the sixties. Kramer and those guys were not big people, but they were quick, they were smart, they never blocked the wrong guy, and they didn't run that many different things.

*Adds **Bill Chance**, one of Vann's teammates:*

We would practice for only about an hour or so. That was all the time we had. Everything was super-organized. You'd go spend ten minutes doing one thing, then quickly move over to do something else for ten minutes.

One thing that was kind of funny was how Vince would explain something about how we were supposed to do something, and there would be Blaik standing nearby in those knickers he always wore and with his arms folded, watching. And Vince would look at Blaik after instructing us on something and say, "Ain't that right, Colonel?" And Blaik would just kind of look away because I don't think he liked Vince saying that to him. It became kind of a local joke among the football players—"Ain't that right, Colonel?"

Chance *also knows the story of how at one point in his career Lombardi wanted to be head coach at West Point and was turned down, only for the tables to be turned a few years later:*

I was back up at West Point from '62 to '65 as a tactical officer and the officer representative for the football team. It was during that time that I heard the story about when Blaik retired [in 1958], they were looking for a new coach and Lombardi, who was an assistant with the Giants at the time, put in for the job. But the school had always had a West Point graduate as a coach. So they turned him down. They said, "No, we want a graduate." And they hired some active-duty guy, although I forget what his name was. He was either fired or forced to resign two years later.

In the meantime, Lombardi had gone to Green Bay and had been very successful there right off the bat. West Point called him and offered him the job, I was told, and he told them no in certain terms that there was no way he would go back there. I don't know if that story is exactly true or not, but I believe West Point could have had him at one time. Now that would have been something.

Hardy Stone came out for the West Point football team as a walk-on:

His most important characteristic was his enthusiasm. He was always bouncing around and moving and had ten times more energy than I wanted to expend at anything, whether it was on a blocking sled or whatever. He thought we should be able to do it a hundred times. He brought out the best in all of us, even in small things.

He had an infectious laugh. He could laugh loud. And he had kind of a deceptive way of looking at you. I think it was a physical thing with his eyes; one of them didn't quite look at you. Both of them were never looking at you at the same time.

Vince Lombardi Jr., born in 1942, talks about his earliest memories of his famous father:

That would probably be West Point. I was in the second or third grade at the time. I'd go to a lot of the practices. I recall him working mainly with the running backs. It was easy to see him because he was moving up and down the sideline, and I could look right up and almost reach out and touch him. He had dummies on the ground, which I suppose were simulating the offensive line, and he would be instructing and exhorting and nurturing and cultivating his running backs.

He never brought much football home with him. He never talked about it. By the time we got to Green Bay, my mother had pretty good insight into the players, their wives, and stuff like that, but she never was one to bring it up with him at home. Dad just wasn't at home much, and even if he was there physically, mentally he was somewhere else. He'd come home for dinner every night, even during the season, and then would go back to work. During the off-season he was still busy playing a lot of golf and would take a lot of trips. He was pretty darn busy a lot of the time.

Vince Jr. on his father's relationship with West Point head coach Col. Red Blaik:

West Point had a profound influence on him. Surely, he considered Red Blaik the finest football coach he had ever been around. Of course, Blaik also worked eighteen-hour days twelve months a year. To be at the [service] academies, you have to be super-organized—you cannot waste a minute.

Lombardi and Blaik were masters at dissecting upcoming opponents and putting together a game plan marked with simplicity, easily implemented contingencies, and room to handle the unexpected; **Jerry Lodge** *takes us through the goings-on for one of the games:*

Our coaching staff was great at developing a scouting report of the opposing team. We already knew what we could do, and the reports showed exactly what the other team could do well.

Let's say it's Duke. One year we played them when they were the second- or third-ranked team in the country, and it was the week after they had beaten Maryland, and Maryland had been the number-one team in the country at the time. So they were very highly rated. Our scouting report showed us that they had an All-American tackle there by the name of Ed "Country" Meadows, a very large kid for that era and a very good player. They also had two good quarterbacks and a running back who was one of the best in the country. And they also had an end who could really catch the ball.

So you go through all of the scouting reports about who their personnel are, what they are likely to do to try to exploit their better players, and what dangers exist in terms of what they're likely to try to do. The next thing you have is *how* do they do this stuff; I mean, what kind of plays do they run? Do they run between the tackles? Do they run most of the time? Do they trap or not trap? Do they sweep a lot? Do they run off-tackle, and if they do, how do they approach it? What about the counterplays? What's going to look like something that isn't? And what's the tip-off that it's a counterplay and not the real play? The Army scouts would have all that worked out, including what would be the splits in the offensive line and when they might line up one way to give a clue if something was going on.

We would have the "B" squad run the plays against the starting defense using Duke's alignments, blocking techniques, and blocking schemes against us. And we would get an idea of what we had to do and how our defense would be aligned, perhaps one way or the other, depending on who the player was that they were opposite and what the scheme was that we expected. We expected a certain proportion of passing on particular downs, so on and so forth. So when I came off the field after, say, the first series of plays when Duke had the ball, the first thing that Lombardi would focus on when talking to me on the headphones was, "Are they lined up the way we expected them to? Do they have the same splits that we expected? Is there any unusual thing going on?" (such as a double flank that we never saw before). The first thing he wanted to know was all about what's different about what they are doing compared to what we expected them to do. And then he would concentrate on trying to get specific changes to specific people. He obviously was seeing a lot of what was going on and would tell me that so-and-so keeps on getting caught inside and therefore the off-tackle play is working because our tackle is being driven inside and not holding his ground. And so you've got to get up the field, get on the outside shoulder of the offensive man, and not let him take him inside. That was a typical kind of thing.

*Lombardi drilled alignments, schemes, angles, and plays so much into his players that they could practically play blindfolded. In fact, sometimes they did just that in practice, as **Peter Vann** points out:*

Blaik had surrounded himself with some pretty outstanding coaches, Lombardi included. After my first season there, I went home for Christmas and came back to school right after New Year's. Now I'm a sophomore, and every afternoon we'd be down there at the field house by four o'clock with shoes, shorts, pads, and helmets, and with wideouts, ends, backs, centers, and quarterbacks. Literally, for two hours every day we went through passing patterns; you know, down and out, down and in, hoop patterns, out and deep. We went through the whole passing playbook and got to a point where Lombardi blindfolded me, just for a down. Being right-handed, I would open [my drop] with a right foot, crossover, plant, and throw. And the end would open with his left, right, left, and plant, and we got the timing down to where you knew where the line of scrimmage was and you knew what a forty-five-degree angle was, even blindfolded. And we were trained blindfolded.

*Perhaps it was because there was too much going on in the way of drills and film study that a West Point player couldn't see Lombardi for the future greatness he would achieve to some degree with the Giants and especially with the Packers. Even without a blindfold, **Vann** admittedly couldn't see the forest for the trees:*

Did I ever have sense that I was in the presence of future pro football greatness in terms of Lombardi? Not for a minute. I think that's part and parcel to the fact that we never realized how good a team we were. We were a bunch of guys who went out there Saturday afternoon and put to work what we had learned during the week, starting on the Sunday morning following the previous week's game. We saw the game films, and the prepper was Lombardi. Lombardi had to not only prep for Saturday, he had to prep for his Sunday morning presentation to the team with the colonel sitting there.

He had to have been up all night getting ready. It was amazing. He would put O's and X's and boxes up on the board so darn fast and he knew in detail every guy. He knew their idiosyncrasies, their weak points, everything. I still don't know when he had the time to study the films to know that when you do a cross on this guy he commits too much to the right but he doesn't commit too much to the left, so if you can cross him to his right, your left, then you could bring a guy in right in front of him and you could score. It was awesome.

I would get quizzed all the time about what everyone was doing, things like, "If you've got a left defensive tackle that is not really charging, what are you going to call?" And blocking assignments. I admit it: I didn't fully know all the blocking assignments. Lombardi sure did. He was a taskmaster for details. Remember the Lombardi quote: "The quality of a person's life is in direct proportion to their commitment to excellence." See, that's Lombardi. He had a commitment to excellence, and I think the only caveat to that statement is when Lombardi would slip down, hitting the negative on his sine curve.

Lombardi carried a lot of this stuff around in his head, and he had a huge notebook. I don't know where in the world that notebook is, but he was writing stuff down all the time. I wouldn't be a bit surprised if that's not his personal playbook. I wonder where it is.

🎵

After Army beat Duke in 1953, Lombardi gave **Vann** *a small gift during an impromptu postgame moment that Vann cherishes to this day:*

I was going to meet some guys downstairs in our hotel to go to dinner. The coaches were on one floor and the players on another. I was on the elevator by myself and the door opened on a subsequent floor, and there was Lombardi. So he and I rode down in the elevator. He reached in his pocket and pulled out five bucks that he gave me. He said, "Peter, go get yourself a beer tonight, but don't tell the colonel. That was a hell of a game." He was more concerned about me telling Colonel Blaik than he was in parting with the five bucks so I could have a beer.

🎵

There was a triumvirate of Mount Rushmorian legends at West Point at one time—Lombardi, Blaik, and Gen. Douglas MacArthur—and **Vann** *remembers it as if it were yesterday:*

I met MacArthur one time. We were playing Virginia, a team we were supposed to beat badly, and at halftime I think it was 7-7. We won, 21-20, in a game in which I had been looking too much for the big-play pass. Riding down the hill from Michie Stadium to the gymnasium complex, Blaik said something like, "Gentlemen, there's a friend of mine that I want you to meet, but I'm not particularly happy that you are meeting him today." We walked, formed a circle in the training room, and in walks Blaik with this guy, about five foot ten and with a black trench coat and black hat. General MacArthur, but without the sunglasses.

He went around to every player and had a comment for him. When he got to me—and once MacArthur's eyes captured yours, you were frozen—he said, "Peter, the probability of a first down is higher when you complete three short passes and then go for the long ball." I said, "Yes sir."

After **Bill Yeoman** *had gone on from West Point to become an assistant coach at Michigan State, he would still run into Lombardi on occasion, mainly when Lombardi was an assistant with the New York Giants:*

At that time in the professional ranks, they used to assign areas of the country to various coaches for them to scout. When Vince was an assistant with the New York Giants, his area was the Big Ten, and I could still remember him coming by and diagramming what would become his "Green Bay Sweep"; I would just start laughing because he would get so enthused and so excited about it. I was afraid I was going to have to carry him out. That was the basis of his offense. He would run that trap as a result of that sweep. You could see a reason for everything that was done with him. He was the same way with us at West Point. It wasn't any great revelation when we called a certain play. Everyone knew what we were doing, and everyone knew why it would have a good chance to succeed. It was never a thing of "Well, the other team is doing this, so we're going to do that," or anything like that. He believed in what he was doing. When guys understand what it is that you're trying to do, that is, understand your philosophy of football, then you can make adjustments while the game is in progress that are very significant. But if you're just running plays for the sake of running plays, then it doesn't work out that well.

Murray Warmath, *a fellow assistant at West Point, said this about Lombardi:*

He felt prejudice. I'm sure of that. He felt that because he was Italian and Catholic that he was not going to be hired by a southern school and a few others, too. And like me, there was nothing else on his mind except being a head coach somewhere.[5]

Former West Pointer **Bill Chance** *said that although Lombardi was an in-your-face yeller, he wasn't afraid of the coach. He even said he really hadn't been impressed with him that much, perhaps because of only being able to look at Lombardi in the context of his being overshadowed by the bigger-than-life Blaik:*

Colonel Blaik had quite an influence on everybody that came through there, coaches and the kids, too. When I first started playing, I was on the freshman team and had about two good games, and the next thing I knew he said to go on up to the varsity. A little later I was out there doing that bicycle thing for calisthenics, where you're on your back on the ground peddling with your feet above your head, and this face looks down at me. It was ol' Blaik and he was looking at me and says, "Are you tough?" Or something like that. I didn't know what the hell to say.

When we went over film, Blaik would do it all. The other coaches might answer questions or make comments, but Blaik clearly was in charge. I think if somebody had tried to act like you might have thought Lombardi would, based on what you saw of him years later, I don't think he would have stayed at West Point. Blaik was in charge, and that was it.

How much of an influence was Blaik on Lombardi? Retired army colonel **Hardy Stone,** *who played at West Point in 1949 and 1950, weighs in:*

I have always believed that nearly everything I saw exhibited in Vince's performance, attitude, comments, and success had the seeds in his experience with Earl Blaik. But at the time I wouldn't have picked Vince as head-coach material. I never saw him react in any way to Red Blaik except "Yes sir, yes sir, three bags full."

West Point defensive lineman **Al Paulekas** *was a vintage Lombardi player, fairly short and stout but with a big heart and a desire*

to hit. Even then, that didn't exempt him from Lombardi's motivational ploys, such as the time that Paulekas suddenly found himself and two other defensive starters demoted before an upcoming game. At least, that's what they had been led to believe:

Evidently, Vince and Blaik didn't like our attitudes or our complacency or whatever it was, so we got to practice one day a week before the first game. For practice the varsity wore black jerseys and the jayvees wore gold, and when I looked in my locker, I had a gold jersey. So did the other two guys. We went out to practice and reported to Doc [Blanchard] because he was the jayvee coach, and he's laughing like hell. He says, "Okay, we're going to scrimmage the varsity," and we put on these padded aprons and were told that we were not allowed to touch the quarterback, who was Bobby Blaik. And Vince was there to protect him.

So when they started running plays wide, we couldn't do anything. And Vince now starts raising hell about lousy pursuit angles and all that stuff, and I looked up at him and I said, "Coach, let us take these aprons off, and then we'll show you some pursuit." And he says, "Nah, we don't want you guys to get hurt." Then three days later we had the big scrimmage, the last scrimmage before the first game, and all of a sudden we had our black jerseys back. The point had been made.

Lodge *saw a lot of Blaik in Lombardi, perhaps even more as time went by:*

What I read about him at Green Bay made him sound exactly like Earl Blaik. In other words, most people played really hard at Army because the last thing they wanted to do was to have Earl Blaik say during the film sessions something like, "Lodge, you were too slow on that," or "Lodge, you missed him, didn't you?" Nobody wanted to hear that. I mean, you are in a darkened room with all of your teammates there on equal footing, and here's Red Blaik, I mean, *the* Col. Earl "Red" Blaik, telling you this stuff. It had to really get through. Lombardi would rant and rave and raise hell and everything else, but Blaik never did. Earl Blaik was the perfect fit for Lombardi. I think he was one of the best things to happen to Lombardi. I think Lombardi learned a lot.

I think what happened is Lombardi absorbed all that, so when he became the head coach he acted just like Blaik did, and in his case that meant dominating grown men. At West Point, we were kind of halfway between a boy and a man in terms of maturity, and, of course, when he got to Green Bay it was a different story. Guys were in the mid- to late twenties and some cases early thirties. But he still dominated them— dominated in a good sense in that he really had your attention, and Lombardi really picked that up from Blaik.

3

LAND OF THE GIANTS

Lombardi finally made it to the National Football League in 1954 on the high side of forty, joining the New York Giants in 1954 as an offensive assistant under Jim Lee Howell. Lombardi spent five seasons with the Giants, eventually becoming half of a coordinators' tandem that ranks as the greatest in league history. Get this: For several seasons Vince Lombardi was the Giants' offensive coordinator, and a young, just-retired defensive back by the name of Tom Landry was the team's defensive coordinator.

Howell would jokingly hint that he was something of a figurehead and content to let Lombardi and Landry run the show, only it wasn't an outright joke. Although Howell had been hired originally by the Giants with the idea that he would the head coach, it soon became clear that the best thing he could do was to stay out of the way while Landry and Lombardi ran the show. Landry was more than ten years

Lombardi's junior, but he had a leg up in that he had at least played pro football. Lombardi never did. Was there an inferiority complex? Doubtful. There were times when Lombardi would yell at Landry's offensive charges coming off the field for what he perceived as letting the team down, although Landry was not the type to reciprocate.

It made sense that Lombardi's entry into the NFL came via the Giants. Wellington Mara of the Giants-owning Mara family had attended Fordham at the same time Lombardi was there, even though they barely knew each other in those days. But Lombardi's coaching pedigree had already been established as far as team management was concerned, although the relatively unknown Lombardi had something to prove to these more mature NFL players, even if he wouldn't have admitted to such. He was a take-charge guy who also was a willing listener, which was a combination that would serve him well among the prominent-playing likes of Frank Gifford, Kyle Rote, and Charlie Conerly.

Dick Nolan, *who would later become an NFL head coach with the San Francisco 49ers and then the New Orleans Saints, was a rookie with the New York Giants in 1954, the same year that Lombardi was a rookie NFL assistant coach:*

I got to know him real well, eventually as a good friend. People always worried about or feared him because he was a tough guy, or they thought he was gonna do something to them. But he was really a pretend tough guy. He wanted things done a certain way, and he was gonna have it done and there was no one that was going to change his mind about it. In so many words he was saying, "Hey, listen, just follow the rules and regulations and everything will be fine. But if you don't, then you'll get your head knocked off."

Although I was on defense and he was an assistant coach, we got to know each other in part because we would go to church together every morning up there in Burlington [actually Winooski], Vermont, where Saint Michael's College is, and that's where we had training camp then. Mass was at 7:00 A.M. What we did was we met right at the door of the church. Most all the guys who were Catholic would go to Mass. Vince always carried a rosary. I did, too, for many years. Sometimes you'd be in there waiting for Mass to begin, and while you were there you'd say a rosary.

Ken MacAfee, an offensive end out of the University of Alabama, also was a Giants rookie the same year that Lombardi came to the team:

It was clear from the start that he had complete control of the offense and ran it with a pretty stiff hand. But he was one of those fellows who could be really tough with you and yet really enjoyed a good laugh.

One thing he did was run calisthenics before practice, and we would gripe, moan, and groan, wondering where this guy had come from. The toughest part was the grass drill, which he would save for the last ten to fifteen minutes of the calisthenics. That was a real backbreaker, but he would always encourage us later by saying, "You'll never run out of steam in the fourth quarter of a game." And that's where he came in with that famous saying of "Fatigue makes cowards of us all." We had had tough workouts at Alabama, but nothing as intense as it was with Lombardi.

❧

Dick Nolan *was one of the first players to work under Lombardi in the NFL, and it didn't take him long to realize that this coach possessed a work ethic a cut above the others in his profession.*

He came in there and worked his tail off all the way through. Whether or not he was thinking he had to prove himself to veteran players or not, I don't know. But you knew whatever he was going to do he was going to do it no matter where he was. If he had gone to Minnesota or Los Angeles or wherever he would have done things exactly the same.

He had to know he was going to get his chance to be a head coach. Consider the fact that we [the Giants] won the championship in '56 against the Bears—we were 14-point underdogs and we beat 'em, 47-7. Obviously, he had a lot to do with that, and that's proof right there he had what it took to be a head coach.

❧

Herb Rich *also came to the Giants in 1954, the same year Lombardi arrived, after having played four years with the Los Angeles Rams. Rich was a defensive back, putting him in position to become well acquainted with Tom Landry and, to a lesser extent, with Lombardi:*

I never really had much hands-on experience with Lombardi, but he certainly was a deep, booming presence on the field.

He taught things in a different manner than Landry did. During film sessions, you could hear him [Lombardi] fussing about and going over some of the faults of his players. You could see that they would get embarrassed, and one time, I remember, it got to the point where, running back Mel Triplett, I think it was, became so fed up with it that he finally said, "Don't play it anymore. Just don't," and he meant it, referring to Lombardi's going over and over a part of the film where Triplett had missed a block.

Landry was different. He was quiet and yet he was the smartest coach I had ever played under as a defensive player. I had four years of pro ball under my belt when I got to New York, at which time Landry was still playing defensive back while also coaching. I could see right away that he really had an understanding of defensive football, particularly in the secondary; his knowledge far exceeded anything I had ever encountered. With him, you knew you had a damn good coach preparing you. Even though I had less exposure to Lombardi, it was clear that he was more of a forceful kind of guy who could inspire you through fear, and fear is a good thing to instill when trying to motivate players, especially those in the pros who sometimes need a good kick. They were both great coaches, and [Jim Lee] Howell was smart enough to let them do their own thing.

At the time, while there was no way that you could foresee Landry and Lombardi becoming the coaching icons, legends, that they became, we knew that they were going to go forward in their profession. After the '54 season, Tom went to the sidelines full-time as a coach. He taught me all about anticipation and thinking out there on the field instead of just reacting to plays. He gave me a broad concept of what the offense was doing and how to anticipate what was going to happen before the ball was snapped and immediately after it was snapped. For example, he taught me that if you saw the wide receiver flaring into the flat and then coming across the middle, that the guy was doing so to take the linebacker out of the inside route and that, as safety, I could look for a pass coming down and in. He was a very, very bright fellow who knew how to impart to players a great knowledge of the game beyond just basic reactionary skills.

Landry was an innovator as well. I believe he was the creator of the 4-3 defense and was running it in New York well before I knew of any other team in the league using it. When I entered the league [in 1950], most teams were playing a seven-man front with two linebackers pulled in tight. There wasn't a need for a lot of spread formations because other teams, outside the Rams, weren't spreading their offenses. Landry with his 4-3 defense was a step ahead of the rest of football.

Although he played offense, **Ken MacAfee** *also got to know Giants defensive coordinator Tom Landry almost as well as he did Lombardi:*

They were as different as night and day, but both men really knew their stuff. Tom was more a man who believed strongly in home and family, where Vince, coming out of Brooklyn and his own upbringing, might have had priorities a little different. Also, Tom was very quiet, and yet he taught me how to play bridge better than I would ever have known otherwise.

I remember one time when Tom pulled me aside to tell me, "You know, Kenny, you almost became a big help to me." And I said, "What do you mean, Coach?" And he said, "Well, if you hadn't made it as an [offensive] end, you could have played for me as a strong safety." I never forgot that.

Former Giants star **Kyle Rote** *on Landry and Lombardi as the top two assistants with the Giants:*

I'd look to the left and see Lombardi in a room running the projector for his plays, and I'd look to the right and I'd see Landry running *his* plays, and then on down the hall I'd look in Jim Lee's room and see him reading the newspaper.[1]

Joe Heap, *who played with the Giants in 1955 as an understudy to halfback Frank Gifford and worked as a return specialist, offers some added insights about Lombardi with some comparisons to legendary Notre Dame coach Frank Leahy, under whom Heap had played at Notre Dame:*

I don't want to be derogatory to [Giants head coach] Jim Lee Howell, but he was more or less a figurehead. Lombardi ran the team with a strong hand and he was always used to having a strong hand. Lombardi was tough.

Frank [Leahy] and Vince both were strict disciplinarians and perfectionists—they expected superlative performance from each and every player. Lombardi was a little wild by comparison, though. He would yell a lot more than Leahy did. Leahy would take you aside and give you a little tongue-lashing, but he didn't have to be as wild as Lombardi to get his point across.

*Linebacker **Sam Huff** offers this take on the Giants' tandem of Lombardi and Landry:*

Lombardi and Landry were quite different, but they worked well together. Back when I was with the Giants, Landry was already putting together a 4-3 defense and Lombardi was just as busy designing an offense that could beat the 4-3 defense that Landry could put up. You just knew they were destined to be great coaches, both of them, and of course both of them are in the Hall of Fame.

Lombardi was the type who liked to have a little bit of bourbon with dinner every once in a while. He drank a little bit, not excessively, but he was just completely the opposite of Tom Landry. Lombardi was enthusiastic; he was a screamer, he was a yeller, and he was an attacker. Landry, on the other hand, would say, "You gotta believe, you gotta believe in what I'm teaching here. I'm going to put you in the right place, but you have to make the play." So he was more the quiet tactician and Lombardi the vociferous attacker. Lombardi would just yell, "Now you go right at that number seventy out there! Go right at him, and we are going to break those guys' wills!" He would just yell and scream. That's the type of offense Lombardi ran: He just didn't give a damn if you knew what he was going to do. He wanted to have his guys conditioned mentally to where they could defeat anybody.

Landry and Lombardi plotted with each other. They worked with each other. They admired each other. They knew they were different people and they worked so very well together. It's my understanding that when Lombardi went to

Green Bay and Landry went to Dallas they took each other's playbooks. Landry developed a defense built around the middle linebacker, and Lombardi's whole offense was set up around the quarterback. Bart Starr was a master at running Lombardi's offense. I don't know if Bart Starr was the greatest quarterback, but he was one of the great quarterbacks because Lombardi had him coached so well. And he knew exactly what to do. One of the things I hated most about playing against Green Bay was their play-action series: Fake the run to Taylor and hit Hornung out in the flat or wide receiver Boyd Dowler going across. They worked on the same plays all the time, and they were so hard to beat when it got down to late in the game.

It had a familiar look. We had Frank Gifford in New York who would run option plays and who was also a good receiver. Gifford never played quarterback for us, although he thought he could. It was a similar situation in Green Bay with Lombardi and Hornung. When Lombardi got there, he took Hornung out of the quarterback's spot, put him in the backfield, and ran the same plays with Hornung in Green Bay that he had run with Gifford in New York.

Jim Lee Howell was as laid-back as Lombardi was intense, and offered this praise of his top offensive assistant:

He was very patient. He would go to great lengths to teach, especially any individual who had promise. The thing that he would not tolerate, that would really upset him, was when a player who had promise let him down—if they failed to do what they were taught. One time a player he liked and respected had this new play down pat and in practice all week he ran it perfectly. Vince was delighted. Then, on Saturday, in our last dress rehearsal, we ran the play over and the player botched it up totally. Vince said very loudly, "You sure messed that up, mister," and the two of them shouted back and forth until finally the player said, "I think the heat's got you." Well, you can imagine! He ended up chasing the player down the field. Lucky for the player he was faster.[2]

Howell on Lombardi's pregame focus:

One night before a preseason game in Oregon, I looked out the window of the hotel where we were staying, and there was Vince pacing back and forth on the second-floor roof that was outside our rooms. He was so intense. We always kidded him after that. When he'd get excited we'd say, "Someone go find a roof for Vinnie."[3]

Former Giants star flanker and running back **Frank Gifford:**

[There was] a lot of competition between Lombardi and Landry, and I don't know if it ever turned into a friendship. That filtered through the team itself. There was tension. We didn't like them [the defense] very much, and they didn't like us as much. And didn't really care. We were cliquey.[4]

AP/WIDE WORLD PHOTOS

Lombardi spent five years with the New York Giants as their offensive mastermind. Here he's pictured in 1958, his last season with the Giants, with (left to right) fullback Mel Triplett, quarterback Charlie Conerly, left halfback Phil King, and right halfback Alex Webster.

Tom Landry:

When Vince and I were together on the Giants, we had such a unique coaching staff in that we had complete control over our segment. Our defensive team was probably a little better received than our offensive team, and that used to make Vince so mad. We'd win a game, 9-0, or something like that, and our defense would come out looking a little better, and he wouldn't talk to me for two or three days.[5]

Lombardi was intense and quick to anger on the practice field, but he also had the kind of sense of humor that would allow him to crack up when he saw or heard something that was genuinely funny without being detrimental to the team concept. **Frank Gifford** *remembers one particular incident in which a group of offensive players, who had been ordered to stand back to await their turn during a drill involving other offensive players, gradually crept too close for Lombardi's liking:*

One day he saw an old beat-up orange peel that had been lying on the field for Lord knows how long. He said, "Everyone behind the orange peel. Anyone who passes the orange peel gets a lap around the field." This sounded so silly that we lined up single file behind the orange peel. He turned around and saw that and roared. Then we all scattered, and every time he turned to watch the play, we'd push the orange peel closer and pretty soon we were right back on top of him. He turned around, began to shout, "I told you guys to get behind the orange" . . . looked down, and here was the orange peel. These were the things that would delight him and crack him up.[6]

Offensive guard **Robert Mischak** *twice played under Lombardi's guidance, first at West Point and then for a short time with the Giants. Mischak remembers one meeting in particular when a short-fused Lombardi was trying to explain some football strategy to rookie players:*

He seemed to expect us to have the same knowledge he possessed. We didn't. He got furious. He ranted and raved and screamed, and we couldn't follow his point, and for a while he just wasn't teaching. . . . He [was] not that sensitive to people. He tried to make me as intense as he was, and I just wasn't that type. . . . To an extent, you had to completely conform your own personality to his, or you were wiped out.[7]

Don Maynard *grew up scared of his father but respectful of his dad's constant admonition to do things right the first time. It was a lesson that served Maynard well when he arrived at Giants camp in 1958 as a rookie out of Texas Western [now the University of Texas at El Paso, known also as UTEP]:*

The one thing that Lombardi would not tolerate was a mental mistake. He'd tell you, "Yeah, you may get beat because the other guy is bigger, faster, or something. But don't ever make a mental mistake." That point was driven into me when Kyle Rote pulled me aside and said, "Study that playbook, know those plays, and don't ever make a mistake, or you're gone."

Well, that's why I made it. There were about five other guys up there with the Giants who had close to the same ability I had, but they blew assignments and stuff all the time. I never made a mistake probably in seventeen years I played, at least as far as a mental mistake. I knew what to do. I knew the right reaction to zone coverage, man to man, or whatever it was because of playing for Lombardi and with all those other guys. We just didn't run the wrong play, period. With those guys on you all the time, how can you run the wrong play? Gee whiz. I never have figured that out. He made everything so simple it's unreal.

In the years since I've done some work consulting with college coaches, and I'm still amazed sometimes how goshdarn hard they make the game out to be. Let me give you an example. Over the years I've learned some stuff about line play from guys like Deacon Jones, Merlin Olsen, Jack Young-blood, and Bob Lilly, and one time I was out at the Touch-down Club at UTEP listening to some coach complaining about how his young offensive linemen were having trouble figuring out what defenses were doing on the other side of the ball and whose man were they supposed to take and all that kind of stuff. So I said, "Coach, when the man's lined up on the center, when the defensive player is lined over the head of the center, that's an odd defense. And when the guy's in the gap, that's even." There ain't nothin' else to it. You see, I'm an old math teacher, too, and there's nothing hard about recognizing an odd or even alignment. Taking it down one step further, when the other guy is on the line of scrimmage, you call him a lineman. When he's standing up a few yards deep, you call him a linebacker. I say I can teach a kid in five minutes how to do things. Don't confuse them. Make it simple. And that's what Lombardi did, probably better than any other coach ever did. That's the way he did it with the Giants.

*Maynard's football career as a wide receiver will forever be linked with that of quarterback Joe Namath during their years together with the New York Jets, although that wasn't Maynard's first stop in pro ball. It wasn't even his first stop in the Big Apple. **Maynard** briefly played with the New York Giants, going there as a rookie out of Texas Western in 1958 and getting a year of seasoning under Lombardi, who was then in his last season as the Giants' offensive coordinator. Maynard reported to the Giants in 1959 but*

didn't last long there, getting cut by Allie Sherman before heading up to play in the Canadian Football League and then returning to the States after the advent of the American Football League. Although he spent only a year with the Giants, the future Hall of Fame receiver left impressed with what he had experienced:

It was probably the greatest honor in the world for me to play on that great Giant team with guys like [Frank] Gifford and [Kyle] Rote, and the great defensive back Emlen Tunnell who took me under his wing. And then on top of that to play on a team that had coaches like Lombardi and Landry. Even then you knew it was something special.

It was a real close-knit group of players, and they had been playing together for a while by the time I got there. They had other guys like Alex Webster and probably about eight or nine other guys that are now in the Hall of Fame. I'm just honored that they still list me in their press guide as one of the members of their all-time roster.

In going to the Giants as a rookie I was the left halfback behind Gifford and also written in as the fifth defensive back. Then they also made me into a kickoff and punt return guy. In those first two weeks of learning all about football knowledge and various techniques, to include blocking, I learned more about football than I had in five years of college. I say five years because I had spent a redshirt year at Rice before transferring. I don't say this to insult my college coaches, but college coaches back then—at least most of them—didn't know about all the finer details of the game to the extent that the pro coaches did.

It was a great year, one I wouldn't trade for anything in the world, not only because I was a rookie around these great players but also because of the great [assistant] coaches they had, coaches who became even greater in the eyes of the public down the road. And I was a student of the game. I wanted to coach someday, and, gee whiz, this was unbelievable.

You could see that Lombardi was going to be a great coach, and I don't just say that because of what we now know in hindsight. Lombardi and Landry were already great coaches. They just hadn't got the publicity or whatever. But you had heard about Landry's umbrella defense and the sweep that Lombardi had put in and made go. One of the things I hadn't realized when I got to the Giants, and which I only read in Gifford's book a bunch of years later, was that Lombardi had really been determined when he first got to the Giants to install the sweep and make it successful, even if at first he had an unwilling audience. Finally, he had a meeting with the veteran players and he said, "Men, I want to make it go. I need your help. I need y'all's help."

The first thing that impressed me about Lombardi was how he would lead his players in calisthenics. When I saw that, I said to myself, "Buddy, let me tell you what, that's what I'm gonna do as a coach someday." Even my son coaching nowadays still does that—leads calisthenics and he's in as good a shape as any of his players.

Maynard learned how to correctly analyze film from watching plenty of it, with Lombardi running the projector and veteran running back Alex Webster as his patient mentor:

Alex really took me in because I don't drink beer. They would give each of us two cases of beer each week, and I'd give mine to Alex. So we'd be sitting together in a meeting watching film after a game, you know, and we'd have to call out the defense on every play, starting with whether it was odd or even. At one point they were calling the defense odd. I'm sitting there watching this, and I turned to Alex and said, "Gee whiz, Alex, that was odd." He said, "No, it's even." So I figured I needed to scoot my chair over a little bit so I could see the film straight on a little better. There were a bunch of times where it was odd, but they kept calling it even. And vice versa.

This went on for quite a while, once a week after every game, including preseason. Finally, one time I said to Alex: "Look, that right there is odd. I could see that guy, and I don't need to move my chair!" Again, he said, "No, that's even." I said, "Why is it even?" And he proceeded to explain to me that even though the defensive guy may line up odd, it's being called even so as to give the proper angle on the blocking situation. I said, "Oh," and sat back in my chair, an educated man.

Frank Gifford on how to humor oneself when around Lombardi:

We used to kid the hell out of him, you know, never letting him forget about Saint Cecilia's and West Point and Fordham. Once somebody dug up a picture of the Seven Blocks of Granite in those funny stances of theirs and it broke us up. There was a game we played called Sports Quiz and the idea was that someone would do a famous athlete and the rest of the guys would try to guess who it was. So once our entire offensive line would get down in that funny old-fashioned stance and yell, "Sports Quiz! Sports Quiz!"[8]

Pat Summerall:

We were training out in Salem, Oregon, that year, in 1958, and I went to the first offensive meeting, and I can remember asking whoever was sitting next to me—I think it was Don Heinrich—"Who the hell is that guy?" because the guy had such an obvious complete command of what he was saying and he had everything down to how long the first step ought to be, how deep the guards ought to pull and, you know, everything like that. It was Lombardi and I'll tell you: He wasn't a backfield coach; he wasn't a line coach; and he wasn't a receiver coach. He was the coach of the offense and he knew every part of the machine—what the ends were supposed to do, what blocks the tackles and guards ought to call. Just a complete command of what he was teaching. What a great teacher he was! I'm sure that in school or wherever you go nine people could say the same thing, but the way that one of them says it makes it stick in your mind far better.[9]

Don Maynard, *recalling one of the Giants practices with Lombardi coming at a player with a full head of steam:*

One day he called this guy over, a tackle, and he yelled, "You big, dumb, blind tackle," and this guy came right back at him with, "Coach, I may be blind but I ain't dumb."

Rosey Brown, *Giants defensive lineman:*

I had a depressed fracture of the cheekbone in '58. We'd tried out a lot of helmets to see if they'd fit properly over the cheekbone, but none of them worked. So Vinnie went home and got one of those old helmets, the leather kind that he used to wear at Fordham. He brought it to the stadium and he said, "Maybe you could use this." It fit, but I wouldn't have dared played in that thing. The point is, though, that the guy was always thinking.[10]

Tex Schramm, *the Dallas Cowboys' longtime general manager, considered Lombardi a good friend, especially in the latter's later years, giving him a unique perspective on two of the game's greatest coaches: Lombardi and Lombardi's former cohort at the Giants, Tom Landry, who would go on to work with Schramm for almost thirty years as the Cowboys' head coach:*

I can't honestly say that I remember Lombardi when he was with the Giants. I knew he was there, but I didn't really have a close personal association with him. I wish I had.

I hired Landry in late 1959, which was later in the same year that Lombardi had gone to Green Bay. I finally got to know Vince because we eventually had him and the Packers come down and play in a charity game that we had here in Dallas. It was a very successful game in those days, and I appreciated his making a spot in his schedule for that. He came down and there were fans who came and pictures . . . but he always helped.

Vince and Tom were two totally different people. I was a very, very close friend of Lombardi's, and we did things and talked about things together. With Landry, it was truly a business relationship. They were two different people, even though they were both Christians. Lombardi was Catholic, and I knew he went to Masses and all that kind of stuff. I don't ever remember that aspect of faith ever being discussed between us; it was just accepted.

Dick Nolan *on the tandem of Lombardi and Landry as coordinators under Jim Lee Howell:*

Tom and Vince basically made all the decisions. They were both brilliant guys. Landry was probably more detail-oriented and an exacting sort of a guy, but Vince was those things, too. The difference was in their personalities. Lombardi was a people guy, and he had a good time with the people and so forth. Landry was more of . . . a little bit of . . . an introvert.

At the time they were together with the Giants it wasn't that you would look at them and think about their future as head coaches. You didn't even know whether they wanted to be one or not. What you did know was that these were guys who knew their business. A lot of times they talked to each other about situations and in trying to find the answers to what a guy on the other side of the ball was thinking. For example, Lombardi might have asked Landry something about defense, what the defensive guy might react to, and what might allow a particular play to go better, and it was the same thing the other way around. They knew their football, they were dedicated to it, and they were great friends.

Lombardi was not averse to helping out a friend in need, and one year he helped Dick Nolan return to the New York Giants after Nolan had been traded, along with Pat Summerall, to the Cardinals following the 1958 season. Lombardi later helped Nolan return to the Giants via the Packers, acting as middleman to help Nolan and the Giants circumnavigate league rules about player movement, as **Nolan** *explains:*

In those days, and I think it might still be the case, you weren't allowed to return in the same year to a team that had just traded you without going through a third team or being put up on waivers. Well, the Giants didn't want the Cardinals to put me up on waivers because they were afraid another team would grab me. That was Lombardi's first season at Green Bay, so he made an arrangement to have the Cardinals send me to the Packers with the idea that he would then turn around and send me back to the Giants. What he said [to the Giants] was, "Hey, let Nolan come up here with me at Green Bay, and after we beat you in the last preseason game I'll trade him back to you."

So I just kind of got my ticket punched in Green Bay. I went up there with Lombardi, worked out with him, and even played a little bit. I didn't play much, but when it came time to play the Giants in that preseason game, he asked me if I wanted to play against them. I said sure. But the first quarter went by and then the second, and nothing happened. Finally, I went over to him and said, "When am I going to get to play?" He said, "Dick, Jim Lee Howell said to 'put that guy back in the locker room and don't play him. I own the guy and I don't want to bust my property up.'"

During the time I was with the Packers, sometimes during practice I would make some big plays out there on defense to thwart his offense, like when he was trying to make a big impression to somebody with how well he was doing with the team. I'd pick off a pass or something and he'd come stomping over and yell at me, "Nolan, you do that one more time and you're not going to go back to New York. You're going to stay right here."

I couldn't tell you how or why we became friends, except I just enjoyed being around him. We'd talk about a lot of different things at different times. When I was at Green Bay with him that short period of time, that was an entirely different situation; I was different to him than all the other players there, even though I was a player. I was the only one there that had known him before he got there, so our relationship was a little different than his relationship was with the other players.

⚿⏀⏀

*Offensive end **Ken MacAfee** at times saw and at other times was the brunt of some of Lombardi's critical rants, but whatever the downside was in the moment, it didn't linger. MacAfee explains:*

Most coaches who chew you out never forget what it is that you did to deserve it. Not Lombardi. He would chew you out for something and forget about it five minutes later. He never held a grudge, not like [head coach] Jim Lee Howell, who would chew you out for something and bring it up again two years later.

Lombardi was able to win over the veterans, even with his tough approach to coaching, in part because he was such a great teacher, especially during our evening meetings. He would repeat himself three or four times teaching us the same thing, and this certainly helped us retain the information. He even told us up-front that he would be repeating himself a lot but that there was a purpose for his doing so and that he was committed to helping us to learn. It showed and it worked.

He kept things simple but put a real emphasis on drilling it into you. And he was great to listen to. Two of the things that I had to learn were his blocking schemes and pass patterns. One of his trademarks was his rule blocking, which applied to almost every conceivable type of play, except for a few special ones. There were three parts to his rule blocking: First, man inside, off your inside shoulder; second, man over, take him whatever way he wants to go; and third, no man inside, no man over, go downfield. These covered almost every contingency likely to occur in a game. I'm talking mainly about his bread-and-butter plays, such as the sweep and off-tackle.

Years later, when he was coaching the Packers, I would watch some of the games and found myself calling every play just from sitting in the living room and looking at the positioning of his players. But it's like what he used to tell us in training camp with the Giants. Addressing the defense, he would boldly say, "Okay, we're going to run the sweep next play, and now it's up to you guys to stop it." He believed there was no way that anyone could stop it.

Before getting the Packers head-coaching job in 1959, Lombardi had time and again experienced the anguish of not getting a top job at a big school or in the NFL, and **Vince Jr.** *could see its effect on his dad:*

There were coaches comparable to him and maybe even some with less ability getting good jobs, and that really ate at him. I think he became pretty frustrated that he'd never get a shot. Having said that, I think there was a lot of pent-up energy as a result of that. I think that by the time he got the job, he knew it was in Green Bay and he knew it was his only shot and therefore he wasn't about to let anything keep him from being successful. Nor was he going to listen to anybody in terms of what to do and how to do it. He was in charge and he was going to do things his way. His being an assistant for so long had prepared him for knowing exactly what he wanted to do.

*Just after Lombardi had made his decision to accept the Packers coaching job, Marie Lombardi pulled Giants owner **Wellington Mara** aside at a Fordham alumni dinner at New York's Waldorf-Astoria. She wanted to stay in New York and pleaded with Mara not to let Lombardi out of his Giants contract:*

She wanted me to stop it. She begged me not to let him go to Green Bay. I could have stopped him. This was at a time when these contracts were sacrosanct. But I didn't. I said, "Marie, I think Green Bay is the place for him."[11]

Mara:

The way we figured it, Jim Lee Howell was going to go on coaching the Giants for a long time. That's really why we agreed to let Vinnie go to Green Bay—and why a five-year contract for him didn't seem constricting. Late in 1959, Vinnie's first year away from us, I could see that the bloom was gone from Jim Lee and I asked him. He said he was tired of coaching. So I called Vinnie and told him the Giants' job was his. He said he would feel guilty leaving Green Bay after one year, to wait another and then the time would be right. So Jim Lee stayed on through 1960, but then Vinnie won the Western title that season and there was just no way he could have come East.[12]

Lombardi was relatively late when it came to being a head coach in the NFL, considering the length of coaching experience he had already logged, but in many ways it was perfect timing for him, even before he got to Green Bay. In going to the New York Giants in 1954, Lombardi quickly became an integral part of a team smack-dab in the middle of the world's biggest media market just as football and television were starting to take off. **Vince Jr.** *remembers those times—the fifties. Until then, college football had been king, and now the balance of power was shifting:*

The Giants were successful then and they were being discovered by Madison Avenue. Television was figuring out how to televise pro football, and the whole thing was coming together. Those were pretty heavy times. Then you had guys like [Frank] Gifford, [Charlie] Conerly, and [Alex] Webster, guys who were heroes to millions. And there I was being in the dorm with them and traveling with them, at least in the preseason.

During the season, my dad and I would drive up [from New Jersey] early in the morning on Sunday for home games at Yankee Stadium. I was still too young to understand fully the impact of everything, but I knew enough to know that being a coach with the Giants meant something and caught people's attention. New York City was a pretty good place to be at that time.

Those drives in with my dad were nice, but even then his mind was elsewhere. It was about a forty-minute drive over the George Washington Bridge out of Bergen County, New Jersey. Maybe he was contemplating the first play they were going to run or how his players were going to handle a certain defense or whatever. Every once in a while he might ask me about one of my high school games, but other than that it was a pretty quiet ride. He and I would have gone to Mass early, with my mom and sister going to church later and then coming into the game later.

4

GREEN BAY AND BEYOND

Confidants of Lombardi had long known of the coach's frustrations over not getting a head-coaching job until well into his forties. He would land an interview here and there but nary an offer, outside of one from the Philadelphia Eagles that he turned down on the advice of his friend and Giants executive Wellington Mara. One story is that Lombardi pined for the Notre Dame job when it was rumored that Terry Brannon was about to get axed after the 1956 season, and he even wrote a letter to the university, but never got a response even after the job did come open in 1958.

If there was one dream job for New York–born-and-bred Lombardi, it was head coach of the New York Giants. Lombardi loved New York. So did his wife, Marie. But he could wait no longer. When the Packers came calling after the 1958 season, Lombardi jumped at the chance, probably thinking he would bide his time for a season or two there before the Giants would come calling for him to replace Howell. That reportedly is exactly what happened after the 1959 season, only for Lombardi to ask the Giants to hold on for one more year so he could leave Green Bay in better graces than bolting back after only one season.

Lombardi never made it back to the Giants, however. After he led the Packers to a dramatic turnaround in 1959—from 1-10-1 the year before his arrival to 7-5 in his rookie NFL season—he took the Packers all the way to the NFL Championship Game. It was a stunning rebuilding effort that in two years made Lombardi the talk of the NFL, or at least certainly the early leader in the unofficial race to beat Landry, who in 1960 had followed Lombardi to the head-coaching ranks with the expansion Dallas Cowboys, to the land of the winners. Green Bay lost that 1960 title game to the Eagles, but the marriage of Lombardi to the Packers had been consummated.

A small country town by NFL standards, Green Bay had quickly embraced Lombardi, and he in turn turned his back on New York and the Giants, deciding to stay in the frozen tundra of Wisconsin because he knew he was part of something special. Marie would have sped back east in a New York minute, but Vince hung in and hung on, ultimately spending ten seasons with the Packers—nine as coach and general manager.

In those nine seasons as the Packers' head coach, Lombardi never had a losing season. Not even close, after his first two regular seasons of 7-5 and 8-4. More significantly, the Packers lived up to an uncanny vow that Lombardi made to his team after its 1960 Championship Game loss to the Eagles—that they would never again lose an NFL Championship Game. Over the next seven seasons, the Packers won all five NFL title games they played in, the latter supplemented by victories in the first two Super Bowls, first over the Oakland Raiders and then over the Kansas City Chiefs.

It was pro football's last dynasty, capped by a threepeat in 1965, 1966, and 1967 that to this day has never been repeated. The names linger: Bart Starr, Willie Davis, Paul Hornung, Jim Taylor, Ray Nitschke, Willie Wood, Jerry Kramer, Herb Adderley, Fuzzy Thurston, Jim Ringo, Boyd Dowler, Max McGee, on and on.

It all came to an abrupt end after the 1967 season, when Lombardi relinquished the coaching reins and spent the 1968 season as the Packers' general manager, only to leave a year later to assume the dual role of coach/GM with the Washington Redskins. As it turned out, that was the beginning of the end for Lombardi. Literally.

Longtime Packers public relations mainstay **Lee Remmel** *was a sportswriter for the* Green Bay Press-Gazette *when Lombardi came to the team in 1959, inheriting a team in disarray following the short and unsuccessful tenure of Scooter McLean, Lombardi's predecessor as Packers head coach:*

Scooter was a soft-spoken, easygoing kind of guy, and he was seriously miscast as the head coach of the Packers, I'm afraid. He had been a very good football player for the Chicago Bears, and I think he was probably a good assistant coach but I don't think he had the capacity to be a head coach. As the great sportswriter Red Smith, who, by the way, was a Green Bay native, put it, in 1958 the Packers "overwhelmed one [opponent], underwhelmed ten, and whelmed one."

They thought it was a little indignant at the time, but in ret-rospect it was a hell of a line.

Then Lombardi came in and one of the first things he said at a press conference was "You'll be proud of this football team because I will be proud of it." People thought, *Who is this guy? I never heard of him.* But he was right, as it turned out.

Hardly anybody in Wisconsin knew who he was. I cer-tainly didn't, and here I was involved in the coverage of pro football to some extent—not as extensively as guys on the beat today. It was a different era then. Information wasn't as readily available then as it is now. I had no idea who he was, to be honest with you. I don't think I really knew who Tom Landry was either, for that matter. All I knew about the Giants was coach Jim Lee Howell, because I had interviewed him in 1957. Lombardi was not even in evidence when I interviewed Jim Lee.

*As hard as it is to believe, considering how **Forrest Gregg**'s notoriety as a Packers player would eventually be so closely tied to Lombardi, Gregg really had no idea what was up when the Packers hired Lombardi in 1959 to be their head coach:*

I had no idea who he was. You didn't have ESPN and CNN and all that stuff then, so different things could happen in different parts of the country and you would never know about it. Or you just never paid any attention to it. There was a big splash up in Green Bay, but at the time I was back in Dallas and all I knew was that we had a new head coach.

Soon after that I happened to run into a friend of mine who had played with the Cleveland Browns under Paul

Brown before being traded to the New York Giants. His name was [Robert] Tiny Goss, and I had played with him at SMU. He said, "Forrest, y'all got a new coach." And I said, "Yeah, we sure do." He said, "Do you know anything about him?" And I said, "No, I don't know anything about him at all. He came from the New York Giants is all I know." He said, "Well, I was there with him for a short time." And I said, "Well, what's he like?" Tiny says, "He's a real bastard." And he was right.

Dominic Olejniczak, *a member of the Packers executive board:*

We gave him a five-year contract at $36,000 a year—which was just what he wanted. We ended up ripping that up and writing it over three times before he left. There were bonuses, too, and when we talked to him about them originally we told him there'd be so much for first place, so much for second, so much for third. He asked if we couldn't include the third-place money, which was $5,000, in the first-place figure, and we agreed to that. He finished tied for third that first year, but we won seven games and he'd done a lot for us. So we gave him a bonus of $10,000. He was so delighted he rushed right out and bought Marie a mink coat.[1]

Fullback **Jim Taylor** *was one of the many great players who played under Lombardi at Green Bay, becoming one of the league's top rushers in the first half of the sixties and one-half of a backfield tandem that also included Paul Hornung. Taylor and*

Hornung were already with the Packers when Lombardi arrived for the 1959 season:

Lombardi came to us knowing exactly what he wanted, how he wanted to do it, and what he wanted to do to play championship football. He was a disciplinarian and a wonderful leader, kind of like a psychologist who just had a knack for being the right kind of motivator for different players. He had a way for dealing with Bart Starr, another approach for someone like me, and still another way of handling guys like Fuzzy Thurston or Jerry Kramer. But you knew where he was coming from, and you knew what he expected of you in order to move to a higher level. He had finally got the chance he wanted, and I think he knew precisely how to implement it.

This team had been a loser before he got here. We had won three games in two years, which is why you can believe the old story about how Lombardi came in, picked up a football, and said, "Gentlemen, this is a football," at which point Max McGee said, "Wait a minute, Coach, don't go so fast."

*After **Gregg** returned to the Packers that summer for training camp, it didn't take him long to get a taste of vintage Lombardi:*

I went up a few days early because I felt it important to get the feel of the new coach and everything. So I rode up there with another guy, a defensive back from Florida, and when we got there we checked into our rooms and told the boy at the front who checked us in that we wanted to sleep late because we were tired, so don't wake us up for breakfast.

At seven o'clock the next morning, we hear somebody banging on the door. It was one of the camp boys and he said that "Coach Lombardi wants to see you over at the cafeteria." So we got up, got dressed, and went over to the cafeteria. It's something I'll never forget. The boy took us over there, and Vince was having breakfast. He got up from the table like a gentleman, smiled, and shook our hands, and I noticed that he was kind of a short guy, with somewhat curly hair and a real nice smile. We told him we were glad to be there, and he said, "I'm glad you guys came early, because now you'll be able to get a little bit better acquainted with the offense and defense. Practice will begin in an hour."

So we went out to practice, and Lord, God, we started off with calisthenics, starting with grass drills where you drop to the ground and then jump back up. I'm telling you what, after about forty-five of those, you are sucking wind pretty good. So I said to myself, *This is going to be different.* Then we went on into the regular practice, splitting up with the various coaches. From that point on, I thought, it wasn't going to be a very tough day compared to those grass drills. A little later, while we were doing offensive line drills, we suddenly heard somebody screaming at the top of his lungs. It was Lombardi, and he was standing over in back of Max McGee. Max had just run a pass route and was *walking* back to the huddle. And Lombardi was giving him the works, yelling, "Mister, we don't walk around here!" And he chewed him out all the way from fifteen yards down the field all the way back to the huddle.

Everybody heard it. And I said to myself, *You know, I may be able to handle this*—because we had heard that he treated everybody alike regardless of what position you played. That was one thing you found out over the years about him. He was tough as hell, but he was fair and he treated us all the same. [Linebacker] Henry Jordan said it best one time when asked how Lombardi treated his players, and Henry said, "He treats us all the same; he treats us all like dogs." Everybody had the same set of rules; there was none of that two sets of rules, one for the starters and one for the guys who were kind of on the back burner. You knew what your boundaries were. And I think that most players enjoyed that, even if *enjoy* really isn't a good word to use here.

Lee Remmel on Lombardi's arriving at Green Bay in 1959, seemingly at first as a square peg in a round hole:

He certainly came from a totally different venue [New York] than what was present here, no question about that; Brooklyn-born, son of a grocer, and now coming to the smallest town in the NFL. That certainly had to be a great culture shock for him. He adapted pretty well over time as evidenced in 1967, the week before the Ice Bowl. He was conducting a press conference and eastern writers were obviously looking for something to put down Green Bay . . . at least that's the impression I got, although maybe I was paranoid about being a small-town guy myself. I forgot how the question was phrased, but Lombardi said, "Gentlemen, Green Bay is a great city, a truly great city." Of course, by then he had been here eight years, but I think he was really fond of the community. I don't know if his wife ever felt that way, but he did.

Recent memories frequently blot out the older ones, which is why many football fans might believe that Lombardi created the Green Bay Packers, when in fact he was being called in to resurrect the glory days of years gone by, as **Remmel** *points out:*

Lombardi's legacy in Green Bay is so strong because it still qualifies as being fairly recent, unlike the legacy of Curly Lambeau. Obviously, many of the people who would have remembered Lambeau are gone. But the fact is that Lambeau founded and nurtured the team and led the Packers to their first six championships. He was the first coach to win three titles in a row, in '29, '30, and '31. He also won over two hundred games, so he wasn't exactly chopped liver. That's one of the sore points with me—that there are a lot of people that have no clue about the past, although I can understand why from the standpoint of the time frames. Yet, there are a lot of people who have no idea that Lambeau, not Lombardi, was the man who founded the team.

Wide receiver **Boyd Dowler** *thinks it was a blessing for all concerned that Lombardi didn't become a head coach [beyond high school] until he was well into his forties:*

All I can respond to is how he was when he was with the Packers and when I was there. I was there from the beginning [1959]. I don't know all about [Lombardi's past and what had prevented him from getting a top job earlier]. Maybe when he was younger, he might have been too abrasive, demanding, whatever. Maybe it was good that he wasn't quite so young when he finally took a team over. Still, he was pretty tough and demanding when he came to us. No doubt about it. Every day was not a picnic, believe me.

John "Red" Cochran, one of Lombardi's first assistant coaches at Green Bay, who came to Green Bay from the Detroit Lions, where he had been let go to make room on that staff for Lombardi's Packers predecessor Scooter McLean:

We knew Lombardi was going to be disciplined because he started with us on Day One. Every day Vince took a certain amount of time that we sat down and went through football just like we were learning it for the first time. He was on the blackboard teaching us with the same techniques that we eventually would use with players. He told us what plays we were going to run, how they were going to be blocked. We were making up our own notebooks at the time, putting all the plays on cards like he had—eight-and-a-half-by-eleven-inch notebook cards with holes in them, just like his bible. I'd call mine my brains. I'd say I left my brains somewhere if I didn't have my notebook. It was Lombardi's brains.[2]

Lombardi in his first speech to veteran players before the Packers' first practice:

Gentlemen, we're going to have a football team. We are going to win some games. Do you know why? Because you are going to have confidence in me and my system. By being alert you are going to make fewer mistakes than your opponents. By working harder you are going to outexecute, outblock, outtackle every team that comes your way. I've never been a losing coach, and I don't intend to start here. There is nobody big enough to think he's got the team made or can do what he wants. Trains and planes are going in and coming out of Green Bay every day, and he'll be on one of them. I won't. I'm going to find thirty-six men who have the pride to make any sacrifice to win. There are such men. If they're not here, I'll get them. If you are not one, if you don't want to play, you might as well leave right now. . . . I've been up here all year and I've learned a lot. I know how the townspeople are and what they think of you men, and I know that in a small town you need definite rules and regulations. And anybody who breaks the rules will be taken care of in my way. . . . You may not be a tackle. You may not be a guard. You may not be a back. But you *will* be a professional.[3]

As bad as the team had been prior to Lombardi's arrival, he didn't inherit a bare cupboard but a team that simply needed a leader who knew what to do with the ingredients. **Forrest Gregg:**

He got a bunch of players who were very talented and, believe me, the Green Bay Packers had been drafting in a good position for several years because they had lost for a long time. There were a lot of great players there who just needed some organization and direction. As an old friend of mine put it, Lombardi put some order to things. As far as the offense and defense were concerned, it wasn't that it was so spectacular and tricky or anything else; it was just the basics. People knew what we were going to do, but they didn't know how to stop us. Same thing with defense: He used to say all the time, "This game, gentlemen, is three things. It is blocking, tackling, it's running. The team that does that best is usually going to win. There's nothing tricky or strange about this business. That's just the way it is."

Fundamentals of the game are the things that carry you through, but having good talent helps that along, because the better athlete you are the better you do these things. When push comes to shove, I think the one thing that he did for us was that he gave us confidence. We had been 1-10-1 the year before he came. And we had no expectations to win. He did. And he got that through to us. He was hard on us and very, very demanding, and he expected you to do the job. It didn't make any difference who you were playing against. Oh, yeah, you could make an excuse like, "Well, I was playing against Gino Marchetti, what do you expect?" and believe me, I got beat a lot. On the other hand, he expected you to not get beat; he expected you to win more of the battles than you lost. That confidence in us made all the difference.

We went 7-5 that first year, even though we always felt like maybe we would have won our division if Jim Taylor hadn't been injured during the season. He was cooking or something or his wife was cooking at home, and they were frying something and he spilled some hot grease on his foot. We lost him for four games. And we always felt that maybe if we hadn't lost him that we might have won a couple more games, and that could have been the difference. Maybe so. Even then, we knew we were going somewhere. There was something good in front of us waiting for us.

*Linebacker **Henry Jordan,** recalling Lombardi's powers, which at times bordered on the supernatural:*

I'll tell you something about Coach. A couple of years back I had this terrible rash on my hand, getting worse and worse. The Packers sent me to five specialists, and they couldn't do a thing. I could see the bone, it got so bad. Even with bandaging I'd be doing pushups at practice and a blade of grass would touch that wound and I'd holler like a baby. One day Coach comes up to me. "Here," he says real gruff and hands me this little unmarked bottle of liquid. "Use this." So I figured, what the hell. Two days later the rash started to heal.[4]

*Fullback **Jim Taylor,** on Lombardi's motivational tactics:*

The players didn't fear him so much as they respected him. It was eyeball-to-eyeball at times, sure, but it ain't like he was going to give you a sucker punch or anything like that.

*Lombardi was still a firm believer in calisthenics when he got to Green Bay, and he didn't let up, as **Taylor** recalls:*

In training camp we had those grass drills where you're jogging in place and you just hit the ground, get back up, and resume jogging in place. He made us do that for two to three minutes. It's a cardio-aerobic type of conditioning. And you didn't get many breaks. He would put you through it to the brink of exhaustion, and then at the end of practice we would run laps around the field and do a lot of forty- and fifty-yard sprints. When he first got there, he was much firmer and consistently stronger, and then after he was there four or five years, he didn't quite have the same drive with us. Perhaps it was because as a team we were getting a little old.

*Bishop **Aloysius Wycislo,** the prelate of Green Bay, who knew Lombardi as an acquaintance:*

In the whole time I knew him I only saw him happy, truly at ease, just once. It was at a party after a football game, and I can't even recall whether the Packers won or lost, but some friends from his Fordham days were in town. They were playing a word game in Latin in which the declined endings were cleverly disguised to score points at one another's expense. Your Latin had to be first-rate to play the game, and Vince was reveling at it. His Latin was excellent.[5]

Marie Lombardi:

When Vin gets one he thinks can be a real good ballplayer, I feel sorry for that boy. Vin will just open a hole in that boy's head and pour everything he knows into it, and there's no way out of it. I don't want to watch it.[6]

Lombardi was not the first great football coach **Willie Davis** *played for. In college he had played for Eddie Robinson at Grambling State before beginning his NFL career with the Cleveland Browns under Paul Brown:*

When I went to Green Bay and I met Lombardi, all at once I met someone who took all of the football fundamentals, all of the training, all of the things that I had been exposed to up to that time, good people, good training, good coaching, and added one other element—motivation! Motivation in that it was almost a personal reason you had to play this game with a certain kind of identity and a certain kind of pride to make sure it represented all the things that were important to you.

As a motivator, Coach Lombardi could put that finishing touch on things about playing a game for a reason, a purpose, and make it reach all the way up to your manhood. If you had it coming, he could get on you in a rough way on the sideline.[7]

Lee Remmel *on his perception of Lombardi's dalliance with perfection and his frequent reactions to imperfection:*

I remember one game in Milwaukee against the Los Angeles Rams. The Packers had a terrible game on offense, and you've got to remember that even though he was now a head coach, the offense was still his personal baby. Green Bay finally won the game, 6-3—two field goals to one. Right after that game he kicked everybody out of the locker room: coaches, trainers, equipment men, his friends from

New York who had come over to see the game. He kicked 'em out of the locker room, and it was just him and the players. He closed the door and let 'em have it. I'll never forget that. The next week they scored something like forty-eight points.

Remmel *on Lombardi, the master psychologist and wordsmith:*

My understanding from the players is that every day during practice week he would say something that would lead up to a final and climactic statement just as they got ready for the game.

Remmel *had been a Packers fan from the time he was eight years old [the mid-thirties] and recalls the Lombardi years in Green Bay as one of his life's finest times:*

No question about it: That was a tremendously exciting time, especially after all those years of mediocrity. I'm not so sure that I really appreciated it all while I was going through it. It's a little different, obviously, looking back from this perspective about those great achievements. But I do think you can take things for granted after three or four championships are won that this is gonna happen forever. It didn't.

Backup Packers quarterback **Zeke Bratkowski:**

When he talked nobody ever stood to the back or side of him. He moved so he could talk to everybody. In our dressing room, he would stand in the middle and everybody was in front of him. And he always talked with notes.[8]

Jim Taylor, illustrating Lombardi's penchant for stressing the basics, over and over and over:

He'd go to the blackboard and put up a play like the sweep, and he'd go over it and over it for forty-five minutes—teaching each player all the little minute things that would make that play work. It was like going to kindergarten where they teach you one, two, three, four, five, A, B, C, D. Just keep it very simple and go over it again and again.[9]

Players never really got buddy-buddy with Lombardi. There was plenty of mutual respect and accessibility, but Lombardi clearly did not belong to the players' fraternity, as **Forrest Gregg** *points out:*

You couldn't really be a friend to him, but you could go into his office any time and talk with him if you had something to say or a question to ask. Sometimes he might come around to see us and listen to somebody tell a funny story or something, but you knew you were not buddy-buddies. He liked his players, but in the beginning we didn't know if that would be the case.

Offensive lineman **Bob Skoronski:**

I remember once he began a speech to us by asking "What is the meaning of love?" And this is what he said. He said, "Anybody can love something that is beautiful or smart or agile. You will never know love until you can love something that isn't beautiful, isn't bright, isn't glamorous. It takes a special person to love something unattractive, someone unknown. That is the test of love. Everybody can love someone's strengths and somebody's good looks. But can you accept someone for his inabilities?" And he drew a parallel that day to football. You might have a guy playing next to you who maybe isn't perfect, but you've got to love him, and maybe that love would enable you to help him.[10]

Lombardi had a knack for telling players, either as a group or as individuals, exactly what they needed to hear to get them properly prepared for the next game or to break out of a personal slump. In 1963 wide receiver **Boyd Dowler** *was having a tough time catching the ball. He was one of his era's best possession receivers, but he could also stink it up at times. Lombardi stepped in with the perfect antidote for what ailed Dowler:*

One of the worst stretches I ever had came along during the '63 season. We were a pretty good team that year, but [Paul] Hornung was suspended that year, and it was one of those years in which we didn't win the championship; the Bears did. Yet we lost only two games that year, and both were to the Bears, who went on to beat the New York Giants for the title.

But it was a strange season for me, individually. Somehow early in the year I got started on some sort of thing in which I started batting around a few balls thrown to me. One of them I bounced up was intercepted by the Bears, and it was a key play in which they ended up winning the game. This went on for about a month, I suppose, where I wasn't playing good and was struggling catching the ball. I got worse before I got better. It's not like we were losing; we were playing pretty well and winning, but it got to where I was kind of scared of my shadow there for a while. It was like I didn't want my number called, which is really atypical for me. I was not sure I could deliver when I was out there.

One thing about Vince was that he would always drive down to the practice field while all the rest of us would walk. It was probably around a quarter-mile, I guess. In practice it had gotten so bad with me that I was just kind of kicking and batting the ball around during practice. I mean, this was my fifth season in the league, right in the middle of when physically you should be at your best. And there was nothing wrong with me, physically. Driving down to practice one day, Coach slowed down and stopped beside me and told me to get into the car with him. He said, "You know, I am not going to pull you out of there. I *could* pull you out of there and put somebody else in, but that would not help matters at all. You go out there and have a good game this week, and everything is going to be fine. But you need to know that I am not going to give up on you, so just get over it. Go out and have a good game and everything will be fine."

He wasn't his usual gruff and dictatorial type self when he said it. He was talking one-on-one. I think that is how he felt about it. It was just a case of a hitter going through a slump, and he knew how to handle it. I got out of that car feeling pretty darn good. I went out on Sunday that week, and I believe it was the 49ers that we played. I caught eight balls for something like 150 yards and scored twice. I had a big day. I was fine. I finished the year with one of the best statistical years of my career. It would have been *really* good if I had caught the ones I should have earlier.

Another time in which I had another kind of bad run was in our first Super Bowl year [1966 season]. We had a little girl that died, a baby born during training camp. She died suddenly. I was pretty hurt, and then I had this little groin problem and this and that. So I was really down; I didn't play well for much of the whole year. I also had a bad shoulder, and that was the year in which I got flipped in the air and landed on my head in the end zone in the league championship game against Dallas. Then I got hurt on the third play in the Super Bowl, which is when Max [McGee] came in to take my place. I was kind of fouled up all year one way or another. It was probably the worst year overall that I ever had. But Coach was good about that, too.

I had my shoulder operated on as soon as we got back from the Super Bowl, and keep in mind this was my ninth year, so I wasn't any youngster. Around February or something like that, he called me in to his office and told me how he knew that I had struggled and that I hadn't played as well as I should have. And he knew that I had been nicked up and that he appreciated the fact that I'd gone out there and tried to play even though I wasn't really 100 percent. Then the fact of our daughter dying. He understood that stuff and said, "Get yourself in shape and come back next year, and you will be fine." That was his way of stroking me a little bit after I had had a couple of bumps in the road.

*Halfback **Paul Hornung,** "the Golden Boy" and one of Lombardi's favorite players:*

Vince really liked my mother. I don't think she ever saw us lose a game and this didn't pass him unnoticed. Like most people in sports, he was incredibly superstitious. It was because of her that I was invited to the Sunday night cocktail sessions at the Lombardis. I seldom went. I didn't want to isolate myself from the other players. One of the few times I did, though, Lombardi was behind the bar. I rushed over and said, "Just one time, mix me something so I can tell everyone that Coach Lombardi made me a drink." And he said through his teeth to me—he was smiling—"I'll be — damned if I'll make you a drink," and then he hurried over to my mother.[11]

*Lombardi the drill sergeant didn't spare the brutal workouts or harsh verbiage with his players, but he didn't beat them into the ground unmercilessly, either. Then again, practice without pads wasn't playtime, as **Forrest Gregg** explains:*

By the time training camp was over, you knew you were in condition and ready to play a full sixty minutes. From then on practice was not that hard because we didn't hit a lot after the season started. We wore pads for a while, and then when it got cold we shucked those football pads and thigh pads and everything and got into sweats, and we wore sweats and shoulder pads and helmets. But whether we were

111

just in T-shirts and shorts or decked out in all our padding, practices were always hard. No exceptions. But they weren't excessively long, either. We made great use of our time. It couldn't have been easy for Lombardi to get that across, because what I found out later as a head coach myself is that once you take the pads off in practice, there's a tendency among players to think of it as play day. It wasn't play day with us; it was still business. We kept our intensity level up regardless of what we were wearing. It was just give-and-take when you came to body contact. You knew how far you could go, and the guy you were going after knew the same thing.

Gregg *talks about how his playing for Lombardi and later under Tom Landry in Dallas helped shape him as a head coach:*

You learn something from everybody that you play for. One thing I do know is that you have to be yourself to be a coach. Before playing that one season for Coach Landry, I had made up my mind that I wasn't going to coach. I figured in order to be successful, you've got to be like Vince Lombardi, and I knew I couldn't be like him. My makeup just wasn't that way. Then I went and played with Tom Landry, and we won the Super Bowl that year, beating Miami in the Super Bowl. Suddenly here's a guy who's successful but totally different in personality from Vince. And I said, "Hey, maybe there's something here that I'm missing."

They were a lot alike in many ways, Vince and Tom. One thing Vince used to say all the time was that there's only three things in your life; your religion, your family, and your job. And he and Tom were on the same page in that regard. Plus the way they conducted practice and organized themselves so well were very similar, perhaps because both of them came from the New York Giant system. But as far as personalities were concerned, they were at different ends of the pole. Tom was a lot easier going, and he didn't yell at you or anything. But Tom expected you as a professional to do your job. And it seemed to me that the peer pressure among players was greater in Dallas. The players knew that they had a job to do and they expected everybody to get it done. You knew in Dallas that every one of your teammates was watching you and if they didn't see you on that day, they'd see you when film time came. Tom would just matter-of-factly point out everything you did well and everything that you did wrong. That was it. If you left the film session after having just been singled out for not doing your job, you could just tell that your teammates were kind of giving you the bad eye. Hey, I didn't do my job. And that's kind of the way it was. That's sort of the story about both of them.

Each of them had their own way, and with Landry there was that unofficial delegation of leadership to the players. He provided the atmosphere or climate for the players almost like an incubator for these guys to develop their own leadership and checks and balances among the players, whereas Lombardi was more like hands-on with everybody, going straight to them with his critiques.

Quarterback **Bart Starr** *preferred his critiques from Lombardi to be in private so as not to weaken other players' perceptions of*

him as their leader, and yet Starr also saw a side of Lombardi in which he could make a good point speaking softly:

His ability to select the most appropriate time to criticize was the factor that made his remarks so effective. During our first year we lost a heartbreaker to a superior team in the final minutes. As we were waiting for his postgame entrance into the locker room, most of the players were dreading what would surely be his tirade. Instead, he calmly walked in and said, "Men, you have nothing to be ashamed of. I know you guys gave it your best shot, and that's what's important. We'll all be better off for it." The team quickly regrouped and went on to finish the season 7-5.[12]

Starr *then gives a counterpoint:*

If Lombardi was surprisingly compassionate in defeat, he could be just as tough on us in victory. After defeating the Saint Louis Cardinals by a huge margin in a preseason game, we walked off the field laughing and slapping each others' backs. When we entered the locker room, however, Lombardi was waiting and quickly brought us back to earth. "Our performance tonight was a disgrace. The only reason we won is because the Cardinals were even worse. You didn't give a damn about playing your best . . . you only cared about that damn score." As he continued his fierce harangue, I thought he must be crazy. When I viewed the game films the next morning, I realized he was right.[13]

*Defensive tackle **Bob Lilly** played for the Dallas Cowboys for most of the sixties and into the seventies, which gave him ample opportunity to accumulate mental notes from the many times the Cowboys and Packers squared off:*

We started playing Green Bay in the preseason in an annual charity game. What surprised me about the Packers was that every year it seemed to be about a hundred degrees for that game and they were in better shape than we were. And I'm not sure whether that was because they were working out in cool weather and then coming down and just having to expend their energy on just one game or what. But they sure were sharper and crisper in those preseason games than we were.

As time went on, I realized how simple their offensive system was. It was repetition, repetition, repetition, and not a multitude of plays. They didn't use a multiple offense; in fact, I think we and the Dallas Texans, which later became the Chiefs, were the first two teams to use multiple offense to any great extent. Anyway, it was a different philosophy and it was sort of interesting, and it would make me think about what it must have been like for the Giants when Coach Landry and Coach Lombardi were coaching together in New York. Coach Landry was always very, very complimentary of Vince Lombardi. He said, "He is very methodical, he's got a lot of character, and he's a motivator." Coach Landry knew that in some areas he was weak, like in motivation. One thing he was, though, was very innovative, I think much more innovative in a way than Coach Lombardi was.

It's sort of ironic how things worked out for them after they left the Giants. Here's Landry, the defensive guy at New York, going on to the Cowboys and coming up with the relative innovation of a multiple offense. I never would have thought a defensive man would have thought of all that. And we had a pretty simple defense, a 4-3 defense—at least it was simple once you learned it. On the other hand, Lombardi, having been an offensive coordinator in New York, went to Green Bay and put together a defense that was relatively complicated. But as an offensive guy, he was pretty much three yards and a cloud of dust.

Another thing about the Packers is that they never made mistakes, and Lombardi kept players who were really *tough*. They weren't mean or anything; they were just tough players. They were very competitive. If you beat them, you had to just physically beat them.

They had about four basic plays they used consistently. They might run them out of a different formation, but those were their bread-and-butter plays. They ran those plays so well that they almost always got a minimum of three yards. They would put you in a third and three or third and two, and that gets very difficult for a defense. They would also throw in a trick play from time to time, and I don't mean just a little first-down pass. And it was stuff not routine for them. It might be an end around or a long pass on third and five—a real bomb. They would totally fool you and do it only once or twice in a game.

Two other things they did particularly well were screen plays and draw plays, and those are two of the hardest plays for an offense to execute. You can easily get caught for a five- or ten-yard loss on a screen play if the defense recognizes it, but it was really tough seeing those plays coming with them, and with us you're talking about a seasoned defense.

Lilly did get to play for Lombardi one time, that being in the NFL Pro Bowl one year. It was a revealing experience, especially because Lombardi didn't have his game face fully on:

We stayed for a while in the same hotel, so I got to know him a bit that way. And he was really jovial and really likable for an outsider like me. The guys on the Packers I talked to still had great reverence for him, but they all said he was a little harsher when he was at home with them. Then again, Landry, too, was very jovial, when he was at the Pro Bowl, but then he was pretty quiet back at home.

Lombardi's Pro Bowl practices were pretty basic. What I remember each day that week is our having a meeting, doing a walk-through for about thirty minutes, then practicing for about twenty-five. His plays were so simple and our defense was so simple that it wasn't hard for guys that were pros to acclimate to that. I do remember that he did give a pretty motivational pep talk before the game, and we had practiced for the game by going over the same stuff over and over and over.

Phil Bengtson, recalling what it was like being Packers defensive coordinator under Lombardi:

I had complete authority of the defense—as complete as you can have—but he was still the head coach. He would come in and discuss football with us, the defense, but not very often and seldom when we didn't ask him to. Oh, once in a while just to pass the time of day he would. He'd hear that projector going, and he'd wonder what we were going to do with this and that.[14]

Henry Jordan about Lombardi's sometimes supernatural-like influence, as in this story about the time Lombardi seemingly got the rain to stop so the Packers could go back out and practice:

We had a longer meeting than usual, figuring we'd never get out to the field to practice, and Lombardi was pretty unhappy, walking around, wringing his hands, looking disgusted with the weather. Finally, he cut out pacing and looked up at the heavens and shouted, "Stop raining! Stop raining!" And there was a huge clap of thunder and flash of lightning, and the rain stopped. . . . I'm a hard-shelled Methodist, but I've been eating fish every Friday since then.[15]

Lombardi yelling at **Jerry Kramer** *for jumping offside in practice, a mistake Lombardi attributed to lack of concentration:*

Kramer! The concentration period of a college student is thirty minutes, maybe less. Of a high-school student, fifteen minutes, maybe less. In junior high, it's about five minutes, and in kindergarten, it's about one minute. You can't remember anything for even one minute! Where in the hell does that place you?[16]

Henry Jordan about how Lombardi worked his team into pristine playing shape with grass drills and calisthenics:

Lombardi shape's when there's no sweat on your jersey in the fourth quarter when you've been in all afternoon. Shape's the guy across the line from you—the sweat dripping and the eyes glassy.[17]

Defensive end **Lionel Aldridge:**

I didn't like the fact that he wasn't very sociable. I wanted him to be more complete and that was sometime missing. But you know, I think part of the reason he wasn't more sociable is that there weren't many people like him and he had no release, nobody to hang out with who was like him. In that sense, I think he might have been lonely. He was a one-class warrior, a one-trick pony in that he had one way of doing things—his way—and it was a right way.[18]

Green Bay's first chance at an NFL title under Lombardi came in 1960, when the Packers played the Philadelphia Eagles in the championship game, which ended 17-13 in favor of the Eagles. Fullback **Jim Taylor** *remembers the final agonizing moments of the game:*

I ended up with the football on the last play of the game. I caught it and was going in to score when I got tackled on about the eight-yard line, and then the guy got on top of me. We didn't have any time-outs left and I couldn't get up and back to the line in time as he was counting down the seconds . . . five . . . four. When he got to one, he jumped and they were victorious.

*Wide receiver **Boyd Dowler** was one of a number of players who stuck it out with the Packers for the nine years that Lombardi coached the team, and he remembers a vow that Coach made after the team's loss to the Philadelphia Eagles in the 1960 NFL Championship Game—a vow that was to be fulfilled:*

After the game everybody was kind of down and hanging their head and this and that. He then came into the locker room and told us that we had absolutely nothing to be ashamed of, that we got beat in a game that we could have possibly won. He then said, "I tell you what: I want you to go home and think about this when you leave here. As long as I am here, we will never lose another championship game. You take that with you when you go home, and you come back next summer and remember what I said and that's what is going to happen."

He was right. That is exactly what he said. I thought about it and thought that was a really great thing to say. It seems like he was always right when you study the big picture as far as our nine years there together with him went.

Some of those things in which he always seemed to be right also included stuff we didn't want to hear. There was a time he stood up in front of us in the locker room after we had beaten somebody and played quite badly—and this after we had won I don't know how many championships—he stood up in front of us and said, "World Champions, my ass. There aren't five of you in this room that could play for anybody else in the league." And we were stunned, looking around the room at each other thinking, *What in the world did he just say, and who are the five he is talking about?* He would do things like that, saying things that really made you wonder, *Where is he coming up with that stuff?* I don't know whether he meant it half the time, because he was pretty darn good at turning on his emotions and saying some things that he might not deeply really believe, but he could make it sound very convincing. He could be very convincing with his speech and with his voice.

He was unusual. He could make you feel so good at one minute and turn the thing around on you the next minute and cut you bad. He was good at it. He could manipulate you a little bit, emotionally, psychologically. I am not sure if he was a good actor or not, like I am not sure 100 percent exactly how he felt, but he sure could make it sound like it was fact, indisputable. He was very convincing. He could also be very emotional, and he could be mean. Sometimes you would think just how mean-spirited a man he was, and then he could turn it around and be warm and nice and congratulate you and laugh with you and everything else. So he could do the whole 360 degrees of emotion on you. Sometimes in the period of one day.

He was amazing. I have never been around anybody like him. I spent time working with Paul Brown when he was with the [Cincinnati] Bengals organization. I was with John McKay at Tampa Bay. George Allen, then with the [Los Angeles] Rams, was one of the first coaches I worked with after I left the Packers. You're talking about some guys who really knew how to win at football, yet there is nobody who I have ever been around who had it like Lombardi did.

After losing the 1960 NFL title game to the Philadelphia Eagles, the Packers came back a year later to crush the Giants, 37-0, in the NFL Championship Game in New York. **Forrest Gregg:**

Before that game against the Eagles in '60 we had worked out inside a gym in Green Bay for two or three days because it had been particularly cold, but we never did that again. From that point on it didn't make any difference what the weather was like, we were playing outside. And of course there weren't any domed stadiums then. We were playing games outside, regardless of the weather, and so we worked out outside. That was a good lesson for us all.

The Packers came back in 1961 and 1962 to win consecutive titles, both of them over the Giants, the second of which was a 16-7 victory at Yankee Stadium in a game that bore some similarity to the Ice Bowl game that would take place five years later [with Jim Taylor no longer on the team]. **Taylor:**

That was a cold, cold ball game up there in Yankee Stadium. It was like twenty or twenty-five degrees below zero. Ice was forming around our eyelids. At halftime I had to get six stitches in an elbow, and I had also cut my tongue, and ended up carrying the ball thirty-one times for something like ninety yards. The wind was really swirling, so you couldn't control passes well. You couldn't cut up the field, and [Giants linebacker] Sam Huff was bouncing me off the sidelines. It was the most brutal game weatherwise I ever played in my career.

Jerry Kramer kicked three field goals in that game for us, and we also scored on a touchdown in which I ran the ball

Enthused Packers led by Paul Hornung (No. 5) and Boyd Dowler (85) celebrate in carrying Lombardi off the field after a 20-17 victory over the Giants in 1961. The victory allowed the Pack to clinch the NFL's Western Conference title, thus earning the team a return trip to the NFL Championship Game.

in. In the game, I ran a bunch of off-tackle plays, and Sam Huff would come in there and say to me, "You stink, Taylor," and then we'd go back to our respective huddles. Late in the game we get inside their twenty-yard line, and Bart hands the ball off to me. I started right and could see some Giants skating around, then saw an opening and cut back to the left and made it to the end zone. I then went over to Sam and said, "How do I smell from here, Sam?"

123

Before **Lee Remmel** *joined the Packers in the early seventies as a public relations official, he had been a reporter with the* Green Bay Press-Gazette. *He had had ample opportunities to interact with Lombardi then, but working with Lombardi wasn't anything like working on the news. Previously, Remmel had covered some dangerous assignments such as murders and strikes. Working with Lombardi, however, was worse:*

During the season he was not the easiest man in the world to be comfortable with. I think he respected me, although we had a couple of run-ins along the way. In the off-season I was the editor of the Packers' annual guide. When I set up my interviews with him, it was just like during the season except you didn't have to be quite as fully prepared. Oh, you still couldn't waste time, but he gave me a fully eloquent and comprehensive answer to every question. I got some great material from him in the off-season, but during the regular season? Forget it. It's unlikely you'd get anything more than monosyllabic answers.

In those days there was no such thing as a Monday review of the previous day's game at a press conference. You would have to call him precisely at nine on Tuesday morning. I had five minutes on the phone. And, obviously, I did have my questions prepared but would still get mostly "yup" and "nope" kind of answers, so I had to do a lot of creative writing. But during the off-season he was a wonderful interview, because then the pressure was off. There was no compulsion to win.

Former linebacker **Sam Huff** *discusses the team-blocking concept characteristic of Lombardi teams and what it was like for*

two teams familiar with each other, Huff's Giants and Lom-
bardi's Packers, to play each other:

What made it so difficult for me was when I came up the
middle. The center would drop off and try to pick me up
coming up the middle. Then they also had a great tight end
in Ron Kramer, who could pick you off, too. They knew
exactly what we'd be doing, and we knew exactly what they
would be doing. So it was a team that hit the hardest, tackled
the hardest, and made the fewest mistakes that was going to
win the game.

That 1962 NFL Championship Game in which they beat
us, 16-7, at Yankee Stadium was the coldest, most miserable
day I ever spent in a football uniform. It was perfect Packer
weather. We had about a thirty-mile-an-hour wind blowing in
zero-degree temperatures, and it's pretty useless having a passing attack on a frozen playing field, which is why we called it
Packer weather. It was the most physical football game that I
have ever been around.

Defensive lineman **Willie Davis:**

I guess as defensive captain I was one of a handful of players
Lombardi confided in at any time. He'd call me in for a personal chat in his office. He knew why I had to play the game
the way I did. When we talked, I understood him and he
understood me. He talked about all the jobs he applied for
and got turned down or never got answers. He talked about
his Italian heritage and its negatives and that he had a great
desire to overcome it. He'd say, "You understand what that's
like, don't you, Willie?"[19]

Lionel Aldridge:

He was different than most people because he could make certain assumptions about a person and know that he was 100 percent correct. He could assume a great deal about a person and know right away if that person would make an effort or be dedicated. He never misjudged me, not once.[20]

Center **Bill Curry,** *who would later become head coach at Georgia Tech, Alabama, and Kentucky:*

Some people can yell at you, and you chuckle because they're ridiculous, the way they do it. But when he did it, it would go straight to your heart, and your heart would go straight to your throat.[21]

Summer camp for pro football players is a grueling, pressure-packed, steamy time as stars work to fine-tune their skills, starters strive to cling to their first-team roles, subs try to knock starters off their perches, and rookies and free agents do whatever they can to make the club. In Lombardi's day, hot fun in the summertime was more like hell, as offensive lineman **Jerry Kramer** *points out in his classic book* Instant Replay, *his diary of the 1967 season. This is an excerpt from his July 25 entry of that year, summarizing Lombardi at his most grueling:*

I spend a lot of time thinking about him these days; I don't have much choice. I wish I could figure him out. I guess, more than anything else, he's a perfectionist, an absolute perfectionist. He demands perfection from everyone, from himself, from the other coaches, from the players, from the equipment manager, from the water boys, even from his wife. Marie Lombardi joined us at a team dinner before one game last year, and the dessert was apple pie. Marie asked the waiter if she could have a scoop of ice cream on her pie, and before the waiter could answer, Vince jumped out of his seat, red in the face, and bellowed, "When you travel with the team, and you eat with the team, you eat what the team eats."

He pays such meticulous attention to detail. He makes us execute the same plays over and over, a hundred times, two hundred times, until we do every little thing right automatically. He works to make the kickoff-return team perfect, the punt-return team perfect, the field-goal team perfect. He ignores nothing. Technique, technique, technique, over and over and over, until we feel like we're going crazy. But we win.[22]

*If **Jim Taylor** were to pick out a flavor to describe the Packers' offensive style, it would be vanilla. Lots of vanilla:*

We were a stereotype football team, but we just overpowered people. We didn't have any finesse, never threw the ball more than about twenty or twenty-five times a game, and even then never threw the ball down the field for more than twenty-five or thirty yards. We were a possession team. It wasn't too colorful, but we kept moving those chains. We'd use up clock getting three or seven points and then let our defense go back out and play for a while, then they would leave it to where we could do our thing again. People knew what we were going to do, but they couldn't stop us. We only had ten or twelve plays, and we ran them to perfection. Our execution level was very high, very good.

Jerry Kramer talks about the thoroughness with which Lombardi coached his players:

After every game we have to fill out reports on the opposing personnel, their ability to diagnose plays, their quickness, their lateral movement, everything. We grade them excellent, above average, average, below average, and poor. When someone becomes available and Lombardi thinks about trading for him, he goes through these reports and gets a lot of valuable information. It's a good bank for him.[23]

*Linebacker **Dave Robinson** came to the Packers out of Penn State in 1963 as one of the first highly touted Green Bay draft picks to get involved in a sort of bidding war with the American Football League. He ended up signing with the Packers when Lombardi accepted his request to get a two-year package worth $36,000—a $12,000 bonus and a $12,000 salary for each of the first two years. One of the lessons Robinson learned from Lombardi was due diligence when it came to talking to the media:*

The lesson learned came in our 1965 game against the Cleveland Browns in the NFL Championship Game. In that game, our cornerback Herb Adderley learned a big lesson for all of us, and it involved what was the only touchdown pass he gave up all year, that being when [wide receiver] Gary Collins beat him for an early touchdown.

What happened is that before the game, a reporter had asked Herb about what the Browns did, and he had told them, "What Collins and [Paul] Warfield do is they go out on a general out pattern; they go hard to the post but they never break off to the corner." Well, that got in the paper, and the first time the Browns got down to around our twenty-five or thirty, Collins ran the easy out pattern and made a hard cut to the post, at which time Herb came in to cut him off at the post. Collins then suddenly broke it back to the corner and beat Herb for the touchdown. Vince Lombardi went crazy, and he told Herb, "That's what you get for talking in the paper, and blah, blah, blah." It was a big lesson for Herb and for all of us—to never say anything you don't want the enemy to hear.

We still won the game, 23-12, and it was Jim Brown's last game. In fact, the Browns had opened up the game with a pass to Jimmy, a play designed to go at Ray Nitschke on the inside, but Jimmy broke it out to the outside where I was, too. They got about thirty yards on that play, and all my friends kidded me about letting Brown get to me for a good gainer on a pass, even though I wasn't primarily responsible.

As could be expected for a coach with such an intensity, Lombardi was just about as hands-on with the Packers defense as he was with the offense. **Robinson** *explains:*

Vince could look at a play or see something, a hole or weakness that had been exploited in our defense. He would go to Phil [Bengtson] and ask Phil, "What was the reason for that hole, or why was it open?" And Phil might tell him something like, "Well, Robinson went in instead of out." And then Vince would come over to me and yell, "What the hell were you doing out there, Robinson? You were supposed to be going in when you went out!"

During practice he would coach defense, but he would check with Phil first just to make sure before he went after somebody. He was never quite sure why the breakdown, even though he could see it. But once Phil told him who it was that had missed something, Vince would give a holler. He was great at being able to anticipate plays and think far ahead about offensive and defensive tendencies.

We were playing the New York Giants in 1967 when they were the number-one offensive team in the league at that time and we were ranked number one in defense. They had [quarterback] Fran Tarkenton throwing to Homer Jones and the whole nine yards. We went up there, and what they would do is bring the fullback, Tucker Frederickson I think it was, out to block me from the inside out. When I would close the seven hole really tight, Tucker would come up inside and then go outside while Homer Jones would be running a fly pattern to draw coverage away. The Giants did that first play of the game and made seven or eight yards, and they ended up running it on me four or five times in the first half, making good yardage on me every time.

At halftime we went in and talked about it, and Vince was livid. Here we were showcasing his team in his hometown. I explained to him that I was closing off that inside hole like I was supposed to and he [Frederickson] was breaking outside. The thing is, I was playing left linebacker, and what I was doing was hitting the blocker at the line with my left forearm and putting my body in the seven hole, and Vince told me, "I want you to play him with your *right* forearm and put *his* body in the hole and keep your body going to the outside so you can play that veer." So I did that the second half and we stopped the play. It didn't hurt us at all in the second half.

The next week, Vince came to Phil in practice and told him, "I want you to run that play at Robinson a thousand times. I want him to see that play in his sleep because he's going to see that play next week." Sure enough, our next opponent had seen the film and they came at us with that play, and we were able to stop it. I didn't have to worry about it anymore. But there's more to this.

About four weeks later we were getting ready to play another game when Vince came to me in the locker room and said, "You remember that outside play?" which we called a 37 outside, I think, and I said, "Yes sir." "Robinson, I want you to get ready for that because you're going to see that play again this week. We're even going to run it on you in practice." And I said, "Okay, but I haven't seen that play in three weeks now." What had happened, and Vince knew this, was that the team we were getting ready to play was the same team that the Giants had played the week after playing us. Vince knew that they had that film from our game, and he figured they would run that play on me. And by golly, the first or second play of the game, here it comes. That was the thing that made Vince Lombardi Vince Lombardi: his knowledge of the game and the way he could predict things.

Another time in L.A., I pulled a groin muscle before the game. I went to Vince and I said, "Vince, I don't think I can play." And he said, "If you don't start, no matter who I put in there to replace you, they'll run more at that guy and break him down. If you can just hang in there, they will test you for the first series, and if you can run with them, they'll go back to the game plan and you won't have to worry about them coming your way anymore." So I said, "Okay." So I go out and on the very first play of the game, here they come with a fly pattern—Dick Bass, who ran about sixty yards downfield. I ran with him and knocked the ball down, and ran back to the huddle. When I got to the huddle, I could hardly walk. If they had come right back at me with the same play, they would've beaten me by fifty yards, but they never came back with it. I got through the game, although I was hurting bad and I had to get shot up again with Novocaine at halftime. That was part and parcel Vince Lombardi.

Backup receiver **Red Mack** *played only one season with the Packers, but it was the right one. It was 1966, when the Packers would go on to beat the Kansas City Chiefs in the first Super Bowl:*

The Super Bowl really wasn't a big thing. We went to Santa Barbara two weeks before the game, and Coach Lombardi told us that this game is bigger than the Green Bay Packers and it is bigger than the NFL. We are winning this game for Art Rooney, for Preston Marshall, and for George Halas, because those were the guys who put the money in to start this league. We're playing this game for them. We were going to win this game and it was important to him. If anybody missed curfew, it was a $5,000 fine. You've never seen grown men stay so close to their locale like that before a game. It was all business, so the game wasn't unlike any other game, and when we went out on the field that day there was no doubt in my mind that we were going to win that football game. No doubt. The game plan for the Kansas City Chiefs was the shortest game plan we had had all year and we had two weeks to prepare. The plays that we were going to run, we were going to score with them. To say that there was one game more important to me than any other game that year wouldn't really be right. The most important thing was just being a part of that organization.

I once had a fellow a couple years after getting out of football who offered me a brand-new Porsche for my Super Bowl ring, and I said no. I wouldn't trade that for nothing. I would never sell it. The Green Bay Packers have always been family, and I'm sure that Vince Lombardi instituted that with that organization. I've been invited back to Green Bay every year when they've invited all the players back for one home game, and not just me but my wife and me. Every year I get a little invitation, and when we get together, our wives are there and the guys have not changed since 1967. They're huggable and they greet you. It's just a warm feeling.

I was born about thirty miles north of Green Bay. And every time I go to Green Bay and drive around Lambeau Field, I still get those old feelings. It's awesome.

Jerry Kramer:

I remember what a thrill it was for Red to come from a team like that [the Atlanta Falcons] to a team like the Packers, and I'll never forget the look on his face after we won the [first] Super Bowl. He was walking around the locker room in his jockstrap, hugging everybody, tears just running down his face, and he was saying, "This is the greatest moment of my life. I just want to thank every one of you guys."[24]

Kramer, in his classic book Instant Replay, *expressed a sort of love-hate relationship with Lombardi, and sometimes the gruff exterior came down:*

I drove downtown to the Packers offices today to pick up my mail, mostly fan mail about our victory in the first Super Bowl game, and as I came out of the building Coach Lombardi came in. I waved to him cheerfully—I have nothing against him during the off-season—and I said, "Hi, Coach."

Vince Lombardi is a short, stout man, a stump. He looked up at me and he started to speak and his jaws moved, but no words came out. He hung his head. My first thought—from force of habit, I guess—was *I've done something wrong, I'm in trouble, he's mad at me.* I just stood there and Lombardi started to speak again and again he opened his mouth and still he didn't say anything. I could see he was upset, really shaken.

"What is it, Coach?" I said. "What's the matter?"

Finally, he managed to say, "I had to put Paul—" He was almost stuttering. "I had to put Paul on that list," he said, "and they took him."

I didn't know what to say. I couldn't say anything. Vince had put Paul Hornung on the list of Packers eligible to be selected by the Saints, the new expansion team in New Orleans, and the Saints had taken him. Paul Hornung had been my teammate ever since I came to Green Bay in 1958, and he had been Vince's prize pupil ever since Vince came to Green Bay in 1959, and it may sound funny but I loved Paul and Vince loved Paul and everybody on the Packers loved Paul. . . . I stood there, not saying anything, and Lombardi looked at me again and lowered his head and started to walk away. He took about four steps and then he turned around and said, "This is a helluva business sometimes, isn't it?"[25]

Paul Hornung, *summing up his sentiments about Lombardi in a 1967 letter he wrote to the coach after learning that he had been picked in the expansion draft by the New Orleans Saints and would therefore be leaving Green Bay:*

I want you to know that I have always felt closer to you than any coach I have ever had or ever hope to have. I believe the greatest thing I have learned from your "Football" has not only been the idea of winning but *why* you want to win! Each and every ballplayer who has had the opportunity of playing under your guidance in some ways will always try to mirror some part of your personality.[26]

Ray Schoenke *of the Redskins, who had broken into the NFL as a Packers rookie under Lombardi in 1965:*

Lombardi is driving and pushing all the time. You have to do it his way. He says we are all creatures of habit, and he builds a team on the basis of constant repetition, something mindless

135

Lombardi demonstrates an isometric drill during the team's 1965 training camp.

we can turn to automatically in a game. His philosophy is we're all kids. Well, it hurts, but it's true. We want the easy way out. Ballplayers are human, and most humans are lazy. I've always been able to get motivated without any outside pressure. With Lombardi, you have to accept the motivation coming from him. It takes a while to get used to that, to forget your own personal pride in being a self-starter, a man with your own code, your own reasons for wanting to excel.[27]

In both 1966 and 1967 the Cowboys and Packers met in the NFL Championship Game, with the Packers prevailing both times in very close games that came down to a late fourth-quarter drive. Dallas tackle **Bob Lilly** *remembers:*

When we played Green Bay in that first playoff game in '66, we watched a bunch of film, probably six or seven games' worth of the Packers. And I don't think we saw them make any mistakes on offense. They got beat every once in a while physically, just like you always do, but they didn't make any glaring mistakes. I think maybe they had an interception or two, or maybe a fumble, but those are just things that go with the game. But as far as blocking assignments and giving things away, they were about perfect. One thing as a defensive lineman you always look for with opposing offensive linemen is if they're giving anything away in their splits or in where their feet are pointing. Green Bay never gave *anything* away. We got something from almost everybody we played, but never from Green Bay.

I'm sure that's an area in which we probably gave some things away because Coach Landry just didn't know the little intricacies of playing the offensive line like Lombardi did. We finally got some of that knowledge when some of their former offensive linemen came to the Cowboys, such as Forrest Gregg a few years later toward the end of my career. I think he was there the year we won our first Super Bowl as a matter of fact. And of course he helped our linemen a lot. He knew all these little tricks of the trade that we had never learned. So Forrest was a big influence, and we also had [former Packers defensive back] Herb Adderley come and play on our defense.

After the Packers' first Super Bowl season of 1966, **Jim Taylor** *was eligible to become a free agent. Players didn't have agents in those days, or at least most players didn't, and so it was up to Taylor to go eyeball-to-eyeball with the general-manager version of Lombardi in negotiating a contract:*

My first contract had been for ninety-five hundred dollars, which I guess was the going rate for the eighteenth player picked in the draft in those days. After a while I got up into the $22,000 to $25,000 range, this after I had been All-Pro four or five years and picked up at least a thousand yards in five consecutive seasons. It was really tough to negotiate and then I played out my options in '66, so I was a free agent. The year before they had signed Jim Grabowski and Donny Anderson to huge contracts, and so the market value of the player had moved up considerably because of the AFL and all. Lombardi offered me a two- or three-year contract to stay with the Packers, and then I went and worked out a more lucrative contract with the Saints. By choice I left.

Tom Landry *had an appreciation for what Lombardi accomplished at Green Bay and how he did it, even if it wasn't his style:*

It was the suffering together that made the Packers a great team. And Vince made them suffer.

It takes a special kind of character to know when to let up, when to back off. He would get them to the point when they were just about ready to do anything, and then he was able to crack a joke or he was able to do something to break the tension and put them back on the right track.[28]

*Probably the most excited **Tex Schramm** ever saw Lombardi was the day before the 1967 NFL Championship Game, which became unaffectionately known as the Ice Bowl. The Saturday before the game was practically balmy by Green Bay standards, with the sun out and temperatures in the twenties. When the Cowboys went over to Lambeau Field for a Saturday practice, Schramm went along and, of course, bumped into Lombardi:*

It was a pretty nice day, and he was so excited when he saw me, because he had installed pipes under the ground to keep the field warm in cold weather. "See how green it is?" he said to me. He also said we were never going to have to worry about cold or anything like that. He walked with me up to the stadium tunnel where the control room was for operating the equipment they had for heating the field. He showed me how everything worked and let me play with some of the levers; he was just so proud and so excited about it. I don't think anybody else had done it at that time.

The next morning when they called me up at the hotel for my wake-up call they said, "Good morning, Mr. Schramm, it is six o'clock or whatever time it was, maybe seven o'clock, and the temperature is minus-something degrees." The temperature was minus two degrees. I looked out and, of course, the place was covered with snow. And those days we didn't stay in a hotel right in Green Bay, because there was too much going on, too much social activity. So now all of a sudden everything is frozen and covered in snow, and here we are trying to figure out how we are going to get to the stadium. Also, here we are, warm, Dallas, southern boys, and I sent one of my guys out and said, "Go by the golf shop and get some golf gloves." He said "What?" not knowing the contingency for our players I was already thinking of.

You should have seen that place. There were people with cellophane over their feet; it was cold. It was about ten degrees below zero, with the wind blowing and creating a wind chill of about thirty-five or forty below. I stood down there on the field, once we got to the stadium thanks to a police escort, and everybody had every kind of sweater, gloves, anything they could find to try and keep themselves warm. My wife and Alicia Landry both sat in the stands. To show you what a nice place it was, some Green Bay people took pity and gave them these snowsuit-like things to wear. So they survived. I was up in the press box, which you couldn't see out of because the moisture from inside was freezing on the window. What I did was get a coffee with some wooden stirrers that I used to scrape off the ice so that our writers would be able to see the game. I was the official ice scraper.

The pipes under the field had gone kaput—they may even have turned them off, I don't know—but it would not have made a difference anyway. I think what might have happened is that the hot pipes might have made things worse because it was melting the first part of the snow, which was then freezing into ice. In the early part of the game it was just a matter of playing in bitter cold, and you could reasonably play a game in that. But by the second half the ground was just ice, and that is why the whole fourth quarter they [the Packers] won the game by putting on a drive that ended up with them only having to dunk the ball over the goal line. We had four or five players that got frostbite out of that game, for which they still have the scars.

Those were conditions not made for our football team. Still, I think that game did a lot to improve our popularity as a team, because it was such a dramatic game and we came so close to winning despite being well out of our element. We were the little guys, and they were the big guys, the big shots.

Linebacker **Dave Robinson** *on the Ice Bowl:*

It was *cold*, very cold. Before the game, Vince was telling us to not feel sorry for ourselves, that it is just as cold for the Dallas Cowboys. "And I don't want to see any of our receivers, defensive backs, or linebackers wearing gloves. I don't want anyone to drop a pass or interception because they're wearing gloves." We didn't have the kind of receiver gloves you have now; all we had were those old [bulky] cloth kind of gloves. I remember telling our trainer, "Here, give me a pair of brown gloves—he'll never know the difference." And I wore gloves out there that day.

Bob Lilly *talks about the Ice Bowl game of 1967 from a different perspective—as a member of the losing team:*

Unlike the year before, we felt very confident because we now had playoff experience under our belts, had gotten many of our players back from injury, and the Packers were hurting with injuries. Plus, we had been playing very well toward the end of the year. We didn't even think about the weather—it never even entered our minds. We knew it was gonna be pretty cold, but when we got there to work out that Saturday it was a soft field and about eighteen or twenty degrees, and that's actually fairly comfortable for a football player at that time of the year. It doesn't really bother you until it gets below zero.

But when we got up real early the next morning to eat breakfast, we saw where it was at least ten below with the wind chill even worse. I looked around at everybody and I could see tenseness—perhaps fright is a better word. We went into the game freezing, and that's something we were totally unprepared for. And we didn't have the proper stuff to wear, and so it's like we froze to death out there. We didn't even have gloves, and here come the Green Bay Packers wearing turtleneck sweaters under their uniforms and using gloves. We made do with things like putting some tape around our ears and cotton in 'em, but we had to be careful about cleaning the icicles from our noses because pulling off the icicles could also mean pulling the membrane of our noses out. There was one game official who in blowing his whistle had part of his lip pulled off. They had to stop the game and give all the officials some Vaseline to put on their whistles. It was just one of those days.

The whole day was a very surreal feeling. Coach Landry looked like a walrus with two icicles hanging out his nose. They were bringing coffee over to us, and four plays later it was frozen. When we first came out, I had noticed these three guys sitting in the first or second row of the stands right behind our bench. I didn't normally even notice things like that, but not only were they real close to our bench, they all had their shirts off and were drinking whiskey. The whole time I'm looking at them thinking, *Man, these Green Bay guys are really tough.* Pretty soon we had to go out on the field, and when I came back to the bench about eight or ten plays later, I looked up to where they had been sitting. They were gone and I never did see them come back. To this day the big question in my mind is if those guys lived or died.

It was a very sad moment in our lives to lose that game, but when we got on that airplane and they got it warmed up and we took off, I was very happy. It felt good to be warm again, and we really had played a great game for those conditions. Down in that one corner where they scored their final touchdown, we were just actually skating around on the ice. That must have been where a pipe broke or something, because the water just settled down in that quadrant and it was just impossible to get any footing.

That game was a test of fortitude, really, and was a testimony to Lombardi's personality. He was one tough cookie with some tough, hard-nosed players, although they were probably the cleanest players that we played. They didn't grab your jerseys. They did all the right things.

Of the few plays that the Packers regularly used in their bare-bones offense, the sweep play with Taylor being led by the likes of Fuzzy Thurston and Jerry Kramer was the most familiar play.
Forrest Gregg:

Key blocks on the sweep were the fullback's block on the defensive end and the pulling guard's leading the ball carrier. Jerry Kramer was probably the best athlete of any of the offensive linemen. He had a lot of injury problems during his career, but he was a fine player.

I ran a single wing in high school and then when I first went to college. I remember the single wing had a lot of pulling linemen—both guards and the off-tackle pulled sometimes. So, with the tight end and guards and fullback all blocking into the hole, the Green Bay sweep was a power play, like the old single wing. And there was the deception of the T-formation. It was sort of a synthesis of the T's quickness and the single wing's power.[29]

One characteristic of Lombardi's Packers teams was their consistency, of which predictability was only a subset of a bigger picture. In all the years that Lombardi coached the Packers to great records and championships, there never was any one player having a breakout season who overshadowed the team. Receiver **Boyd Dowler,** *an embodiment of that characteristic, explains:*

I was pretty consistent. That is one thing you can say about all of our players. There was never anybody that had what you call a really bad year. Some years were a little better than others, but none of them would you ever consider saying that anybody went out and had a really bad year. We had a couple times when we didn't play as good overall as a team as we should have, but it wasn't by a significant margin.

Coach Lombardi handled things pretty well. He didn't always do it by screaming at you. He did it by *dealing* with you. He was a real human being about it. He understood, I think, just exactly how far to take people. He knew how much he could scream and bark and holler. He knew he could get on a horn anytime. Every one of us had our own way of dealing with it. He could holler and do anything he wanted, and Paul [Hornung] would just shrug his shoulders and say, "You're right, whatever." And Jerry [Kramer] would get mad for a while, temporarily, and fuss around a little bit and stuff like that, but none of this really hurt him. Coach found out early, however, that Bart [Starr] wasn't the kind of guy he could scream at in front of everyone else, with his being the quarterback and the leader of the team. Bart didn't respond to that. Lombardi understood early on that if he had something that he had to tell Bart, he would call him into his office and sit down one-on-one.

Lombardi was a smart man who understood his players. He understood one thing and one thing only, which was that he had to get us playing to the same level of excellence that we were capable of. That's the greatest thing he ever did. Over a nine-year period, he took the nucleus of the football team, which was the same guys who were there from the beginning or almost the beginning, and got the same performance out of people in 1967 that he had gotten out of us in 1959 and 1960. The same guys played the same way when they were older as they did when they were young. He was always able to motivate us. Some teams have a Super Bowl hangover—it happens all the time, but it never did happen with us. We won two titles in a row once and won three in a row another time. A couple of other times we came awfully darn close to throwing another one in there. In '63 and '65 we were an awful good football team. We probably should have won three in a row then, but we didn't do it. Really, our only down year in there was '64, but then we bounced right back and won three in a row. There was an awful lot of very good football being played by that team for a period of nine years.

*Defensive lineman **Willie Davis** could see Lombardi as more than a one-dimensional man:*

There was definitely another side to this man. He could get teary-eyed talking about life and the reasons for things happening like they do. As the defensive captain, I was sort of the liaison between him and some of the players. A guy came to me—Bob Jeter—he had one of his relatives pass away, and in those days we made so little money, just barely enough to make it, literally, from week to week and through the offseason. This was early on in camp, and he [Lombardi] came to me and said, "Look, here's air fare for Bobby, and I don't ever want to hear anything else about this."[30]

Tom Landry:

He believed in winning as strong as anybody I've ever seen. Yet he was someone you'd find in church, going every morning before starting the day. That is going to have an effect on one's behavior and you saw that in Vince. He believed no one reaches his or her potential unless they're driven to do so. I think that Green Bay Packer team learned to hate him because he overworked them. A lot of times that hatred becomes love when you're successful, and those guys loved him.[31]

Landry, after the Packers had beaten his Cowboys, 21-17, in the famous Ice Bowl game of 1967 to win the NFL Championship:

The discipline and conditioning programs they went through, the punishment and suffering, they all tend to develop character. And once you get character, then you develop hope in all situations. That is the great thing that comes out of it. And Vince developed a lot of character in his players, character that a lot of them probably would never have had without the leadership and discipline he developed in them. Therefore, they never were out of a game. They never felt like there wasn't some hope. And that is what carried them through to that third championship. That is what beat us.[32]

Forrest Gregg recalls the Ice Bowl:

We knew that maybe there might be a weather advantage to us because we had been up there and we were comfortable playing with the weather in the twenties in Green Bay at that time of the year because we worked outside every day. But when I woke up the next morning and found out it was like fifteen below, I said, "Oh, my God, I can't believe this."

The field was not frozen when we started the game, but as it progressed it got more solid and more solid all day long. When we finally got down there on the goal line at the end, man, there was no traction. Neither team had any traction. We tried a couple of plays that didn't work before Bart went to the sideline and came back in with the play. A quarterback sneak. We ran the sneak, scored, and that was it. I give Dallas a lot of credit because they came from the weather down there the way it would be in January compared to being in Green Bay in January. Both teams played exceptionally well, and it could have gone either way. You know, we could have been stopped on that one-foot line and it would have been all over.

Boyd Dowler on the Ice Bowl game, in which he caught two first-half touchdown passes that had staked the Packers to an early 14-0 lead:

The Ice Bowl was the most memorable game I was ever involved in. The circumstances made it kind of bizarre when you get right down to it. What we were dealing with at the time was the whole motivational thing about trying to win a third straight title. And an Ice Bowl victory against Dallas in Green Bay would put us in the Super Bowl.

For some reason we never had any doubt that we would win the Super Bowl, if we got there, those first two years. But the hurdle in 1967 was getting through the Cowboys, as it had been the year before. Then to show up that day and have the temperature be sixteen degrees below or whatever. The day before had been kind of overcast, but other than that there had been nothing wrong with it, at least not for late December in Green Bay. Even the field was quite manageable the day before; we practiced on it and it was fine, and, boy, you show up the next day and find this.

How the game was played and then how it all came down to the end was something truly unforgettable. It came down to the very end and the last time we took the ball, where the whole thing was kind of tied in to the nine years' experience of playing for Coach Lombardi, with our taking the field with about four minutes left and trailing [17-14], and the whole nine years and a third consecutive title weighing on one final drive. You know you go out on the field and have four minutes.

Lombardi didn't change a thing for that game. He didn't say anything different and didn't do anything different. When we got the ball back toward the end of the game for that last possession, he and Bart decided to go back to some of the things that we had done much earlier in the game. When we went in for what we knew would be our last-chance drive, we were going on some information that had worked for us earlier in the game, and that was dropping off the ball to the side for our running backs. There was a little bit of a plan going on for that last drive based on some information on what had worked earlier in the game and some information that worked for our running back that dropped the ball off at the sides.

Despite the weather, we tried to run the same game plan we had already put in. But between the time we scored those first two touchdowns and then got the ball back for that last drive I don't know how many first downs we had been able to convert. I doubt if it was five; maybe closer to two. We hadn't done anything. Bart had gotten sacked something like ten times. Then he fumbled it once and they picked it up and ran for a touchdown. Then Willie [Wood] dropped a punt, which he never did—although in that weather it's amazing he caught any of them, and from that they kicked a field goal. Otherwise all Dallas really did on offense was that big [option] pass play to [Lance] Rentzel [for a touchdown]. On the other hand, we did nothing between when we scored our second touchdown in the second quarter and when we got the ball late in the fourth quarter. We did absolutely nothing on offense. I don't remember if we went three and out every time, but it seemed like it. It was awful.

Then we went out there that last time, and it was like, Well, so here we are—we had better do something. There was never any doubt in anybody's mind what we were going to do. And for some reason it just kinda happened, but that's kinda the way we were. You get to where you just know how to win, and you figure out what you need to do and then you just go about doing it. But Lombardi really didn't say a whole lot, even at halftime. We had only been doing it for nine years now. It's the case of what you do is what you do. But that game to me was the climax of our whole nine-year existence there.

Jerry Kramer, referring to a 1967 playoff game against the Los Angeles Rams:

In the locker room, before the game, Coach Lombardi took his text from one of Saint Paul's Epistles. I don't know which one. Maybe Vince was just using Saint Paul's name to back up his own theories, but anyway he said the key phrase was, "Run to win." Coach said that many people enter a race and just think about finishing or about coming in second or third, but that when we enter a race, we're only looking for one thing: We run to win. Vince has a knack for making all the saints sound like they would have been great football coaches.[33]

Lombardi's pregame pep talk to his team before they played the Oakland Raiders in Super Bowl II:

It's very difficult for me to say anything. Anything I could say would be repetitive. This is our twenty-third game of the season. . . . Boys, I can only say this to you: Boys, you're a good football team. You are a proud football team. You are the world champions. You are the champions of the National Football League for the third time in a row, for the first time in the history of the National Football League. That's a great thing to be proud of. But let me just say this: All the glory, everything that you've had, everything that you've won is going to be small in comparison to winning this one. This is a great thing for you. You're the only team maybe in the history of the National Football League to ever have this opportunity to win the Super Bowl twice. Boys, I tell you I'd be so proud of you that I just fill up with myself. I just get bigger and bigger and bigger. It's not going to come easy. This is a club that's gonna hit you. They're gonna try to hit you, and you got to take it out of them. You got to be forty tigers out there. That's all. Just hit. Just run. Just block and just tackle. If you do that, there's no question what the answer's going to be in this ball game. Keep your poise. Keep your poise. You've faced them all. There's nothing they can show you out there you haven't faced a number of times. Right? . . . Let's go. Let's go get 'em.[34]

There's likely no way Lombardi would have taken any NFL head-coaching position offered if it didn't come with the added power of general manager. Lombardi wanted, needed complete control of football matters to completely shape a football team in his image, and giving him those two hats to wear was the only way he could be accommodated. But the sixties introduced a growing proliferation of agents and a signing war with the upstart AFL, among other headaches, which ate away at Lombardi's

151

*power to control contracts and bully players into accepting salaries well below their requests. The changing environment was no more evident than in 1966, when Lombardi was forced to offer a deal well into six figures for University of Illinois star full-back **Jim Grabowski,** who was being heavily pursued by the AFL. When Grabowski was asked to meet Lombardi in Green Bay to discuss a contract, Grabowski's agent, Arthur Morse, made Grabowski promise that no matter what Lombardi said or offered, he would say he needed twenty-four hours to think it over. But Lombardi, in person, was still a formidable force to a starstruck rookie:*

Lombardi, without hesitation, looked me right in the eye and said, "Here's what we'll offer you. We'll give you a three-year contract. The amount is four hundred thousand. You can split it however you want. . . ." He looked me right in the eye and said, "What do you think, son?" And I, without thinking, shook my head yes and said, "Sure." My attorney is hitting me under the table to remind me of the twenty-four hours. But I couldn't help but say yes. That's it. Let's get it over with. . . . The look, the trophies, the pictures of the team, the legend, how can you not be influenced by this? I should have known then this was the first sign of the great psychologist that he was.[35]

Vince Jr. *on his dad's retirement following the 1967 season, explaining it as motivational burnout:*

Anybody who motivates and gets people going sooner or later runs out of things to say. You've got to take your act to a new

Lombardi in his final training camp as Packers head coach, screaming at one of his rookies to push that blocking sled a bit harder.

venue. What's he going to tell these guys to get them to reach down and do it one more time? They'd done it five times now. I think he saw that coming. I don't think he bailed out because he saw the inevitable decline so much as he just figured, what's the point?[36]

After Lombardi announced he was leaving Green Bay to take over the Washington Redskins, Wisconsin State Journal *sports editor* **Glenn Miller** *wrote:*

153

It is true that our hero has treated us rather shabbily at the end. Vince Lombardi has gone off, without asking us about it, and made himself a deal in a foreign land to the east. He has cast us aside, rather roughly at that. It is probably true that our former idol has been crafty, calculating, even a little deceitful with us.[37]

Ben Starr, *Bart's dad, wrote the following letter to Lombardi after the latter's retirement as Packers coach:*

It is with a feeling of deep gratitude that we say "thank you" for all you have done for Bart since he has been associated with you. He gives you the entire credit for any and all success that he has had, and we know he is going to miss the meetings he has shared with you, but we are thankful that you will, at least, still be associated with the Packer organization. I and my wife both feel that Bart will probably rely on you to still offer him advice. It is not only because you are the finest coach in football, but the type of religious man you are also that has made us so happy for Bart to be associated with you. He admires you in so many ways that you have had a far deeper impact on him in more ways than you will probably ever know.[38]

Chuck Mercein *recalls Lombardi's coaching "sabbatical" of 1968, the year between his relinquishment of the Packers coaching job and his move to Washington, a year in which his lone role of Packers general manager kept him close to the action but not really a part of it:*

He made a real mental error, a real mistake in judgment in leaving coaching in the first place. I think about two or three weeks into training camp . . . he realized it. He was sort of lurking about, peeking around corners, seeing what was happening, and very reserved about it, wouldn't show himself too much. And once the season started, he looked tragic, no other word for it. Just tragic. And when he came to Washington, I understand he told the team at Carlisle, "The reason I came back is because of you guys." The players. I think he [believed] that.[39]

Chuck Lane, then the Packers' public relations director, recalls trying to develop a media campaign for Lombardi's successor, former defensive coordinator Phil Bengtson:

When Phil Bengtson got the job, I felt we should look for things to try to build Phil's reputation and why Lombardi had chosen him. So I proceeded to publicize the fact that Phil's defenses had never finished below second in comparative league statistics. I thought it would make Phil look better. The minute after that release was on his desk, Lombardi came through that door full speed. He reminded me—in no uncertain terms—that it wasn't *Phil Bengtson's* defenses, it was *his* defenses and that Phil Bengtson was merely implementing or installing them.[40]

Tex Schramm's take on why Lombardi left Green Bay to take over the Redskins:

155

I don't know exactly why he left the Packers. I think it was a surprise to a lot of people when he announced he wanted to coach again because I really thought he didn't want to coach anymore. But you also seem to forget that he was still a pretty young man. He was only about fifty-six or fifty-seven when he died. He was just tired of being up there, in Green Bay, I guess. It was a pretty confining place. He figured he couldn't do it anymore.

Vince Jr. *on his father's return to coaching in 1969 with the Redskins:*

I think he was tired and worn out, and I think the pressure had kind of gotten to him, but he had been enticed over the chance to have a percentage of the team's ownership.

I can recall driving down the street with him in Washington when he turned to me and said, "You think I made a mistake coming back, don't you?" I said, "What the hell are you talking about? I never even thought about it. Why are you asking me? What the hell do you *care* what I think?" Actually, I hadn't really thought about it much at all. But I think he had some doubts. If he thought that it was important enough so as to bring it up to me, then I'm sure he had some doubts.

My last memory of him, obviously, was seeing him in the hospital right before he died. My dad didn't want to admit that his time was ending, so we never did have any of those end-of-the-line conversations. Tomorrow never came for us. And I wasn't one to bring it up. So, that's just how it goes.

Chuck Mercein, who was brought to the Packers by Lombardi in 1967 and who later followed the coach to the Redskins:

In a way Lombardi was Green Bay. Who else was there? Everyone was obsessed with Lombardi, but in the end they got used to him. Here, they're not used to him yet. The Redskins ask me all the time, "Was he this way in Green Bay? Has he always been like this?" . . .

It just tickles the hell out of me to see somebody smile from ear to ear the way Lombardi does, just like it scares the hell out of me to see somebody get as mad as he does. And I've seen him on the edge of tears through anger, where he can hardly talk, and, well, when you're used to him, you react to him. You react strongly to his emotions. The game can be a pleasure and a misery, but you're involved, you're reacting.

You see, Lombardi thinks football is all about emotion. Some coaches have gone so much to technique and science that they've taken the personality and fire out of their players. Not Lombardi.[41]

Boyd Dowler's reaction to the news that Lombardi was quitting as Packers coach:

I wasn't that surprised when he said he was gonna do that because his goal had been to win three in a row, and besides, we were getting older and we were going down. That was not our best football team. The year before was not our best football team of the whole nine-year period, either. None of

It is February 1969 and Lombardi has just told the Packers executive committee that he is resigning as general manager to become head coach and general manager of the Washington Redskins.

those last three teams were our best team under Lombardi. Other teams were catching up to us physically, so it was no surprise when he left. And it really wasn't much of a surprise when he left a year later to take over the Redskins. I never believed he would stay long in Green Bay as just general manager. He wasn't happy doing that. It was obvious he wasn't happy here.

*Wide receiver **Max McGee,** after the third consecutive title and Lombardi's retirement as coach:*

After we were winning a lot, it was easier on the players but harder on him. And it got to the point where there was nothing more left for him to do in Green Bay. I mean, three titles in a row! Another thing was maybe that he wanted people to know he was the reason for our continued winning. I mean I loved the guy, but you have to say he was very egotistical.[42]

Count Packers linebacker **Dave Robinson** *among those not surprised when Lombardi came out of coaching retirement in 1969 to take over the Redskins:*

I was surprised to see him retire, but I was not surprised to see Vince go somewhere else. I had been on the negotiating team for the '68 players association contract when he was just a general manager. We talked and I knew it was eating him alive not to coach football. I knew he wanted to coach football. I tried to figure out how he was going to get around to telling Phil Bengtson that he would not coach the last two years of his contract and would instead take back over the defensive coach's job while he [Vince] returned as head coach. Vince couldn't sit on the sidelines too much longer, and then he went to Washington and that's what surprised me—that he would go someplace else.

Lee Remmel *on Lombardi's decision to step down as Packers coach following the 1967 season:*

I couldn't look into his mind to determine exactly why he decided to step down. I do think he was physically and emotionally drained after that '67 season because he really drove himself to win that third one in a row, which nobody had done in that playoff system. He also deeply resented the advent of agents, and they were becoming a problem as far as he was concerned. A third thing is I think he really felt that the responsibilities of a general manager were becoming more and more difficult, and that they would demand more of his time. That eventually turned out to be the case.

His secretary [Ruth McCloskey] said subsequently that the summer of his general managership he would walk into her office and say, "Ruth, what am I going to do this afternoon?" She'd say, "Why don't you go out and play golf?" and he'd say, "I did that yesterday." The very first day he walked onto the field as general manager only, he knew he had to get back to coaching. But he said, "What could I do? I couldn't take the job back from Phil Bengtson because I'd just given it to him the year before."

*As hard-nosed as he was and coming out of a background in which players were expected to be totally sacrificial to the concept of team, Lombardi understood that bucking the players union wasn't in his best interest. When he got to the Redskins, Lombardi soon met receiver **Pat Richter,** who was the team's player representative to the NFL Players Association:*

We would have occasional conversations about matters regarding player relations, and you've got to remember that those were contentious times [circa 1969] in terms of trying to get things organized with the players association. But he always respected that and respected the fact that being true to the players association was part of my responsibility and that he would not get in the way of that thing. That continued on to the next year and until when he was ill.

Richter wasn't surprised by the demands Lombardi placed on his new team in 1969—his reputation had preceded him:

Coming from Wisconsin, I was well aware of what he had done and accomplished in Green Bay. I knew that he was very tough but fair as a motivator and someone who philosophically had little things that he said that had meant a lot to the people who had played for him. There was a little bit of trepidation and fear, because of that reputation and the unknown. Just how tough was he? The workouts, the grass drills; very efficient. He didn't waste any time on the practice field. The other thing was that if you had something like a muscle pull, you tried to take care of it yourself. You didn't want him to find you in the training room. And the first meeting we had, we learned that Lombardi time meant being ten or fifteen minutes early, so that if someone came in five minutes early they were actually late.

He made it clear that if everyone does his part to be successful, the enterprise will be successful and will be rewarded as such. But if somebody breaks down and is sloppy or careless, the whole enterprise will break down. What he was really driving at is that's the way life is. If you do it here, you might lose a football game, but if you do it out there as a fireman, policeman, educator, lawyer, or whatever, then the stakes would be much higher.

Try as he might, Lombardi could not hide the fact from the Packers players during the 1968 season that he missed coaching on the sideline. **Forrest Gregg:**

I saw him when he'd come to practice. He would just sit over there, and you could see him chewing at the bit to get into the action. It didn't surprise me that he went to Washington.

Perhaps Lombardi regretted his move to Washington, as **Lee Remmel** *speculates based on a conversation he later had with a close friend:*

Even when Lombardi was still fairly healthy, there was some talk that he was thinking about coming back to Green Bay. At least that's what a close friend of his, a former vice president of the Packers, said. He told me that he had visited with Lombardi that year and that Lombardi had indicated he'd be receptive to coming back to Green Bay. Obviously they are both long gone so we can't document that, but that's what this man told me and I had no reason to doubt him.

Ray Schoenke *of the Redskins didn't take long to find out how painful it could be playing for Lombardi:*

Just before the season started, I tore a ligament in my chest and everything I'd fought for went down the tubes. The pain was just terrible. I've played with all sorts of hurts, but this ripped ligament was the worst thing I've ever endured, just excruciating. Lombardi was going to get rid of me. The bluntness of it all. The fear that he meant it about cutting me. The panic that he was going to jot down in his little mental book that Schoenke couldn't take it, wasn't mentally tough enough, was unreliable. His philosophy was: If you can't do it, I'll get rid of you and get somebody else. He believed that. He actually believed he could get somebody else, even after the season started. So he was fearless, completely fearless.[43]

Schoenke, a left tackle, knew that no matter how well he played, week to week he would always have to prove himself worthy to Lombardi. The psychological pressure to do the right thing under Lombardi's watchful eye could have a player playing mind games with himself, as Schoenke recalled a 1969 game against the Baltimore Colts in which his likely on-field rival would be Colts defensive end Roy Hilton:

I studied Hilton backward and forward, was really up for him. The game gets under way, and [tackle Jim] Snowden is having a lot of trouble with Bubba Smith, so [coach Bill] Austin told me to be ready to take Snowden's place at right tackle. So I'm on the bench trying to think how I'll work Bubba, then [guard Willie Banks's] ankle's going fast. So they want me back in at left guard because Billy Ray Smith's having a field day, beating Banks to the inside. I felt like a juggler, thinking about how I'm going to work on three different guys, and I know I've got to keep concentrating on the guy I'm playing against right here and now. I knew I couldn't get rattled, couldn't make a mistake, had to show

Lombardi I could execute. I had a pretty good day at Baltimore as both a guard and a tackle.[44]

Offensive guard **Vince Promuto** *of the Redskins, recalling how Lombardi was just as tough from the get-go with the Redskins as he had been with the Packers:*

I figured I was a tough [guy] and nobody was going to get me down. That first day in Carlisle I found I was wrong. I was ready to say uncle. Lombardi didn't stop until everybody was bushed. And you weren't used to him, you never knew how much longer he'd make you do those damn ups-and-downs. You'd lie on the ground and say, "This guy's a madman, he'll never stop," and within fifteen minutes you were bushed, frightened to exhaustion, and you had to do the next one hour and fifteen minutes on courage alone. This is his idea of getting you ready for the fourth quarter. Not even the Chinese could do so well at breaking you that first week.[45]

By the time Lombardi arrived in Washington, Redskins quarterback **Sonny Jurgensen** *was in his mid-thirties and nearing the end of a career that had been noteworthy and often individually productive with prodigious passing numbers, most recently under Lombardi's failed predecessor Otto Graham, himself a former quarterback. Jurgensen needed someone to push him to another level of excellence, and Lombardi fit the bill:*

We've all got hope now. There never was that feeling under Graham, not even at the beginning. We were an explosive team in those days, but we were not a sound one. Now the people who've been pampered on this team in the past because of their exceptional ability, the people who just tried to get by—they've been forced to change. With Lombardi, cheating is out. You don't rest up for one play on the field and then put out on the next one. You don't run a pass pattern one time and not the next, block one time and not the next because you know the play is going away from you. With Lombardi, you do it every play, on every situation, or you won't be out there the following week.[46]

One of the first relationships Lombardi made it a point to culti-vate when he first got to Washington was with Jurgensen, the prematurely potbellied free spirit who had long since established himself as one of the league's premier passers. But there's a gap between being just a great passer and a good quarterback, and Lombardi preferred the latter, as **Pat Richter** *point out:*

Lombardi had a great relationship with Jurgensen. His primary thing was that he made sure Sonny was the focal point and the leader, and that everything worked through him. In that respect, everyone knew so much about the success of the Packers' offense and defense—how it was simple and straightforward and it was all about execution. Nothing fancy. Because the Redskins hadn't had a winning season in something like ten seasons before he arrived, a lot of it was attitudinal. He had been successful where he came from, and he felt good about doing the same kind of thing with the Redskins.

🏈

Sonny Jurgensen:

I played for nine different coaches, but the one year with Lombardi was the high point of my career. I worked harder that year and had more fun than any other year. . . .

He could diagram a play on the blackboard and say, "Now there's no way the defense can stop that." And you'd believe him. Then he'd leave the room and tell an assistant to draw the same play up in left formation. The assistant would draw it up, and you'd say, "There's no way that play can work."

It was just his ability as a motivator. He was a teacher. He knew how to motivate individually. He'd ask of some, demand of others."[47]

🏈

In taking over the Redskins, Lombardi faced a similar task to the one he had taken on in 1959 when he took over the Packers—turning around a moribund franchise. **Pat Richter:**

Because of what the Redskins' record had been like over the past ten seasons, most of what Coach Lombardi tried to do with us was to reinforce the positive things about doing the best you can, playing as a team, and doing all those things. And if we had confidence, he could put us in a position where we would be able to win.

If he had lived beyond that first season, I think he would have been more successful long-term than George Allen was after he came in [in 1971, after Bill Austin had replaced

In going to Washington, Lombardi inherited the chance to work with Redskins quarterback Sonny Jurgensen, one of the game's finest passers at the time.

AP/WIDE WORLD PHOTOS

Lombardi for the 1970 season]. George traded a lot of the draft choices because, as he said, "the future is now." I think Lombardi would have built a more solid base for the long term—he would have been more selective and not given up as many draft choices.

After we won our first game that year, there was a tendency for us to come into the locker room after the game thinking that everything was wonderful and Coach was going to tell us how we did a great job and all that. But he just tore us apart in our first meeting after we had won. Then after a game we lost, we thought he was really going to get after us, but he didn't. It was a reverse psychology. He knew your mind was receptive to what he was going to say after you lost, but when you won he really got after you because he knew if you made the same mistakes in another game you might lose that one. The fact that we had won the game was now gone, it was in the past, and you had to be thinking about the here and now and what was to come.

In the meetings you paid attention to what he said and how he said it. I also remember that there was a priest in training camp all the time. Mass was said every day. You could see the priorities Coach Lombardi had in the way he carried himself. You saw the results and it was a great motivation. Had he been there a longer period of time, I think he would have been just as successful as he had been with the Packers. He even tried to help us a little bit in that area by bringing in guys like Bob Long and Chuck Mercein, who had been with him at the Packers and through whom he could sprinkle some of that success on us.

*Running back **Larry Brown** came to the Redskins in 1969 as a rookie halfback, although that positional status soon changed:*

I was a halfback, but I was blocking pretty good, too. I guess it was the blocking that caught his eye, 'cause one day I walked into the lunch room, and the rookies were supposed to stand up at their table and introduce themselves and say where they went to college and what their position was and sing their school song. So I stood up and said, "I'm Larry Brown from Kansas State and I'm a halfback, and now I'm going to sing you my school song." And as I caught my breath to start in singing, comes this voice: "You ain't no halfback anymore, Brown; you're a fullback now." And it was Coach Lombardi, and it kind of surprised me, and I didn't sing my song too good. Fullback? Hell, that kind of worried me.[48]

Lombardi didn't let up much on himself between his retirement from the Packers after the 1967 season and his move over to Washington starting with the 1969 season. **Pat Richter** *explains:*

Now that I look back on that year he coached us, even when we were on a trip or even just going from the stadium to the airport on the bus, he would fall asleep because he had given everything he had, and now that the game was over it was total exhaustion. He had totally spent himself.

Redskins defensive back **Pat Fischer** *was an ace at reading quarterbacks and pretty good at reading Lombardi as well:*

Lombardi is a salesman. He has to sell us on winning. Each day he sells the team. He's leading up to the right moment to clinch the sale, and that's supposed to be on Sunday. That's the day we buy. . . . It's hard to sell forty men week after week. Damn hard. Probably impossible to get to all forty. Maybe thirty's all you need, maybe thirty-five. You just can't be sure, so you have to shoot for forty. I have the feeling that each day Lombardi tries to think of some little story or parable he might tell that will stick in your mind all week, make you susceptible for the Sunday sale, sort of like a car salesman pointing out a new accessory every day. Lombardi's all design.

Lombardi is clever, and he always couches his words positively. He never speaks in negative terms during the week, like most coaches do. Where they might say, "We can't have any more interceptions, we can't have any more of this damn fumbling, we can't have these break-downs in the line," Lombardi will go at it the other way. He'll say, "We've got to throw the ball just as accurately as we did in the second quarter, we've got to continue opening up those big holes like we did in the third quarter." After Tuesday, he doesn't remind you of the mistakes you've made.[49]

Fischer was in his ninth season as a pro during Lombardi's one season with the Redskins:

I don't know what the word is for the feeling you're supposed to have about your coach. Respect is not quite it. But whatever it is, Lombardi has it. . . . He makes no bones about being all business.

And there is a paradox there, too. I'll have to admit it. If you can be traded to help the team, then bam, you're gone. Yet, you're supposed to have loyalty toward the team and the coach, and you ask, where is the loyalty that's supposed to be flowing back to me? . . . It's bothered a lot of people. And how can you expect to remain stable emotionally under such an arrangement? You can be gone tomorrow, yet you're supposed to have this strong feeling about the Washington Redskins. Well, it's a problem. He's talking about very lofty, noble things, but how do you instill them when the underlying concern is insecurity?[50]

Larry Brown, a Redskins rookie in 1969:

He never treated me like a rookie. After he knew who I was and after he'd been watching me awhile—when he began paying any attention at all—he treated me like a veteran. I was just out of college and he was on me like I was a third-year pro, yelling at me the way I suppose he yelled at Paul Hornung and Jim Taylor. Once he chewed me out so unfairly—I thought so, anyway—that I began to hurt inside. I was hurting with hate for this man. Three or four days later he came up to me again—just as unexpectedly and for no better reason that I could see—and he put his hand on my back and said, "Good play. You're going to be a good boy."[51]

Added Fischer:

I contend that Green Bay didn't win its championships because of that part of Lombardi that shouted, drove, and criticized. The Packers won because of the personality you don't read about, the part you see when he's joking. He can be damn funny. It's peculiar, because his jokes are usually terrible, but he puts so much of himself in them, he's so determined that they're going to be funny, that they are. Maybe that's his real personality. The screaming is all put on, his way of moving people and getting something out of them. You have to get to the point where his yelling doesn't affect you, drive you into the ground. But until you know him, the yelling and all is the only way he has to motivate you.[52]

Vince Promuto:

I figure if you play with Lombardi long enough, love doesn't sound so fruity. You're talking about forty ballplayers who have learned that respect for each other. The kind of love Dr. [Martin Luther] King was talking about.[53]

Boyd Dowler *was an assistant coach with the Los Angeles Rams at the time of Lombardi's death in 1970, with the season just getting under way:*

I knew he had been real sick, and it was pretty obvious that he was gonna die. I heard about it on the news, but didn't go to the funeral. Training camp was finishing up, and I was told that someone else would represent the Rams and that I had to stay there. I should have gone anyway. I just should have done it, and I didn't, but that's a different story. We all have our regrets, believe me.

5

ASSORTED MEMORIES

Along with everything else, Lombardi had a commanding presence. Relatively short and squat, he could stroll into a room filled with senators, CEOs, and cinema celebrities and instantly draw center-stage attention. He could also cry at the drop of a hat or bite somebody's head off at the drop of a pass. Grown men didn't just love him one minute and hate him the next; they could do both at the same time. There was nothing neutral about this guy; nothing bland, few things forgotten.

He was a man of contradictions as well as convictions. Bold about his love for God and his embrace of his Catholic faith, Lombardi could yet spout profane language bluer than a sailor's. He was usually a paragon of humility and respect around women, yet once terribly embarrassed Marie by chewing her out in front of his team for asking for a dessert otherwise forbidden to his players at a team dinner.

Lombardi preached the team concept to his players every chance he got, which was about every three minutes, yet there was an egotistical side to him that took credit for all those victories and championships. When Lombardi's handpicked successor as Packers head coach, former defensive coordinator Phil Bengtson, once answered critics questioning his worthiness as coach by pointing out that his defense had been ranked second in the league three times running, Lombardi exploded, saying that it was *his* defense that had been so distinguished.

In the end, Lombardi made quite an impression. Lots of them, in fact.

About the same time that **Tex Schramm** *and Lombardi were becoming good acquaintances, in part because of the growing rivalry in the mid-sixties between the upstart Cowboys and the dynasty-laden Packers, they became members of the same team as original members of an NFL committee that would oversee the rules of the game. The off-season meetings provided an environment that made for some good times, especially considering the variety of exotic locales and the occasional golf games, as Schramm remembers:*

Sometime in the sixties the league created a competition committee that was supposed to get together and make the rules for the improvement of the game. This was right about the time of the merger with the AFL, although we weren't necessarily involved in meshing their rules with our rules. That was the deal. But this was a pretty strong committee made up of some pretty strong individuals: There was Lombardi, Paul

Brown, Al Davis, and me. We got to know each other real well because of the time we spent together, which in those days was for about a week at a time. Those meetings were very productive in those days. We made rule changes or whatever we felt necessary, such as what to do with the draft—we tried to make the game better, whatever the area of the game. Even Al Davis. Everyone on that committee was committed to doing anything that was good for the game, if not necessarily good for them or their particular team. There weren't very many people that were going to question those people.

As chairman, it was up to me to decide each year where we would go for the meetings. I always tried to find different places that were nice and offered a change of scenery. One time we had a meeting in Jamaica and another couple of times in Acapulco. Then there was Hawaii and, of course, Palm Springs.

One time while we were meeting in Hawaii, we went out and played golf because Paul Brown was a real ardent golfer. He loved the game. Lombardi was an average golfer but not really that good. We tried to get Al Davis to play, but golf was never his game. This one time we were playing we got to a par-four and were walking up on the green getting ready to putt. And all of a sudden a ball came sailing in on the green. Immediately, Lombardi turned around with his club in his hand and started running back up the fairway toward the group that was playing behind us. He called them everything that he could think to call them for hitting into us. Actually, he got halfway back to them before he finally turned around and came back. But, oh man, was he cursing; he was so mad.

So we finally get to the next hole, which was a par-three, and of course, one of those short holes you usually had to wait for people to putt off. So we waited and hit our shots, and we get to that green and are getting ready to putt. All of a sudden, this guy in a golf cart from the group behind us starts yelling, "Mr. Lombardi, Mr. Lombardi!" Vince looked over there and said, "Those SOBs, if they want to say something to me then I am going to go over there and they are going to get theirs!" So Vince starts over toward them and the guy on the cart says, "Mr. Lombardi, you left your putter on the last green. Here it is." Not a sound. Vince just stood there and then said, "Thank you," and he turned around and came back. It was so funny because he was so mad, and nobody knew what he was going to do.

There was another time over there when we were playing these two new courses over on the big island. After the meetings got over, we decided we would go there and spend a week and play golf and relax. So my wife went there along with Vince and his wife, Marie. Vince and I were out on one of the courses playing while our wives were off doing something else. At one point we hear a woman yelling off in the distance and look over to another fairway, and we can see that it's Marie in a golf cart, charging toward us yelling, "Vince! Vince! We've got a grandson, we've got a grandson!" And that's how Vince learned he had a grandson.

After the meetings and golf, all that was left to the day was to watch the sun go down in a place like Hawaii or Jamaica, and that's when **Schramm** *saw Lombardi most at peace and in awe of the beauty the world had to offer:*

He had a room that faced the ocean, and we had a room across the hall that faced one of the big volcanic mountains. Every night we'd go over to his room and drink and watch the sun go down. It was beautiful, the kind of nice experience that I have never forgotten.

As a West Point cadet playing under the taskmaster Lombardi, there rarely was the occasion for social interaction, so quarterback **Gil Reich** *left his West Point days behind not really knowing his coach and certainly not realizing just how much of a part Lombardi would play in his life later on:*

Other than the practice field, the practice sessions, team meetings, and games, I didn't get to know him on a social basis until many, many years later. After I graduated from Kansas and spent two years as a commissioned officer in the air force, I joined a company in Chicago in the middle fifties and spent ten years there, and then I got transferred to Milwaukee in 1965, where I became a manager for the Equitable Life Insurance Company. He was then coaching the Green Bay Packers, and they played half their home games in Milwaukee.

The first thing I did as the manager of our company there was get in touch with Coach Lombardi—it was either by phone or by letter, I don't remember—and he was very, very kind. The first thing he said to me was, "You need some tickets for our games in Milwaukee and in Green Bay, don't you?" and I said sure. So he got me four of the finest season tickets you ever saw. After their first NFL Championship season, they had a big sports night at the Milwaukee Athletic Club, and he and the team came down for the black-tie affair, and he invited me to sit at their table. During his after-dinner speech, he not only recognized me as one of his former quarterbacks at West Point, but he also wanted the audience to know that I was a manager for the Equitable, and that if they wanted to work with a great insurance company and buy some great insurance, they ought to work with Gil Reich. Now how's that for an endorsement! You can't pay for that kind of advertising.

From that point on, I never had any problem hiring agents or selling insurance in Milwaukee. We were up against Northwestern Mutual, which is a great company in their own right, so I couldn't have bought that kind of endorsement for a million bucks. All I could think was how gracious this man was and how considerate he was, how loyal he is to his kids, whereas at West Point he had been as hard as rock and as tough as nails on us. And now, some years later, about fifteen years later, he was still supportive of us but in a different way.

Lombardi was a tough guy but with a big heart. He was very emotional, very religious, although he could be really hot-blooded in stressful situations, especially on the gridiron. But he was great for me, and I will never forget what he did for me.

Vince Lombardi Jr. has long walked in his father's shadow, but he forged out a career as a motivational speaker, adhering to and espousing many of the same principles his father had outlined:

He would exude confidence; it was easy for the players to have confidence in him and his system. He was passionate about what he did. Part of that was I'm sure just something that he developed, but I think part of it was God-given. I think he had an electricity about him, an intensity about him, and a focus about him of which some of it had to be inherited. Some people are just born with that stuff.

My dad was one of those men who just had great presence. When he walked into a room, you knew it. After a while his reputation preceded him, but he had this quality even long before he had become well-known and could easily be spotted out of a crowd. I can recall any number of times when my dad would be out of town and wasn't due back until, say, Thursday, but then he might get home early on Wednesday. And he would walk into the house, and you just knew he was in the house, even if you didn't see him come in. It's not like you actually felt his presence, but somehow the atmosphere in the house had changed. It was just that intense. And, again, some of that I'm sure is God-given. But some of that is developed, too, and it comes from knowing your strengths and your weaknesses and playing through your strengths.

*President **Richard M. Nixon** at a White House dinner paying tribute to Lombardi after Lombardi's death on September 3, 1970:*

[Vince Lombardi was a] man who in a time when so many seem to be turning away from religion was devoutly religious and devoted to his church; at a time when the moral fabric of the country seems to be coming apart, he was a man who was deeply devoted to his family; at a time when it seems rather square to be patriotic, he was deeply and unashamedly patriotic; at a time when permissiveness is the order of the day in many circles, he was a man who insisted on discipline . . . discipline and strength.[1]

Ethel Kennedy, Bobby's widow, met Lombardi at a surprise birthday party thrown by Washington Post *editor Ben Bradlee and his wife, Toni, for Redskins owner Edward Bennett Williams in 1969:*

He was like a rock. Everything in his philosophy and his life reaffirmed my childhood beliefs. Seated next to me was a man—with that marvelously toothy grin—who was expounding on the need for competition, desire, drive, discipline, and pride. I remember thinking this is how a mountain climber must feel when he reaches the protective overhang of a rock. Always the image of a rock—and then it clicked . . . one of the Seven Blocks of Granite. His presence was so overwhelming I forgot who else was in the room—except for one other person, Marie. The conversation at our table came around to Vince's toughness. Much to my surprise, from about six seats away, Marie's penetrating voice shot across the table: "Everyone thinks Vince is fierce, hardboiled, temperamental, and ruthless—when in truth he's just a bunny!" I asked Vince if he thought that particular image of him occurred to his players. He said he didn't think so.[2]

Vince Jr. on his combustible relationship with his dad:

With me he was pretty free with the back of his hand, but five minutes later it would be forgotten. . . . But my father and I really had some classic blowouts, no question. He'd never say, "I think it's raining. You'd better wear your boots." He'd say, "Get out of here with your boots on."

Christmastime in the Lombardi household in 1967 finds (left to right) daughter-in-law Jill Lombardi, grandson John, Vince Jr., Marie, grandson Vincent III, and Vince.

The last really big thing we had was back in New Jersey. I slammed the door, and he came out after me and I hit him. He'd been on me for quite some time, and I just hit him before he did anything to me. He was really shocked. He went back into the house, and he came out and was ready to do me in. He wouldn't have knocked me down, only cuffed me. And my mother was really trying to keep him away, and I could hear the shuffling of feet and my father saying, "Get out of the way, let me at him!" and my mother saying, "Oh no, remember what you did to him last time."[3]

Marie Lombardi, *on her husband's taste in music:*

He was crazy about music—didn't know a lyric, but he was crazy about music. And Sinatra! His special favorite. We went to a Sinatra show in Miami, and Frank insisted that we sit on stage. And the introduction he gave Vinnie! It was very special. Frank sang "My Kind of Town" that night, but Vince said later that as far as he was concerned Frank could have substituted "New York" for "Chicago" in the song. He never stopped loving New York. Neither have I.[4]

Packers linebacker **Dave Robinson** *saw Lombardi as the consummate motivator:*

I give sales talks two or three times a week, and I used to wonder what Vince Lombardi would say to these people right now to motivate them, because back in those days he always motivated us every day, and he always had something new and fresh to say. He would say the same thing to you a thousand times a week in a thousand different ways so it was always fresh and new, and he always fired you up. I had other coaches who would tell you the same thing a thousand times the same way every time. That's not very inspiring.

Another thing that made Vince so different was his and Marie's tradition of having a Thanksgiving Day dinner for the team every year. All the families came and the children went down to the basement, where they could watch cartoons while a babysitter took care of all the kids. The adults were all upstairs for a little cocktail hour before they brought the families up, and we all sat down family style and had a

Thanksgiving dinner. The only requirement was that when dinner was over, you were expected to take your whole family by and meet Mr. and Mrs. Lombardi, and what this did was allow him to meet the wives and keep track of the progression of family members in terms of numbers and growth. Oh, and we were also told before the fact that no player was to drink more than two beers at the dinner. Until just five or six years ago, my wife, Elaine, hadn't known about the two-beer rule, and she had always thought that I was just doing right by my own by not doing much drinking.

Television sportscaster **Howard Cosell:**

I'm a superb gin player. He didn't think he was bad, but I'm watching him and he's beginning to lose. He knows I've got a photographic mind and he's getting increasingly disturbed. So the other guy gins, and Vince turns around and says, ". . . will you get the hell over to the bar and have a drink? I can't stand having you watch me. I know what you're thinking." I just roared. And I threw that incident up to him for the rest of his life. He just couldn't stand being seen in an area where he wasn't the best. He couldn't stand it. So every time I'd say, "Hey, Vince, you wanna play a round of gin?"[5]

Red Mack *was an NFL journeyman who found new life with the Green Bay Packers in 1966. His journey around the league was significant from the standpoint of the reception he received with the Packers when he joined them for one season. Mack*

played for Lombardi during the 1966 season—when the Packers went on to win the sport's first Super Bowl:

I was drafted by the Pittsburgh Steelers in '61, went to Philadelphia in '64, back to Pittsburgh in '65, and then got picked by the Atlanta Falcons in the expansion draft. But before the season started, I got released by the Falcons. It was on a Sunday. They simply told me to bring in my play-book and then I left, driving back home to South Bend, Indiana [where he had played for Notre Dame]. I woke up Monday morning and my wife told me that Pat Peppler, the Packers' personnel director, was on the phone and he wanted to talk with me. So I went downstairs, and he said, "Vince Lombardi would like to talk with you." So he put Lombardi on the phone and he said, "Red, we've picked you up from the Atlanta Falcons. You're now the property of the Green Bay Packers. When can you get here?" I said, "When's the next practice?" He said, "Tomorrow morning at nine o'clock." I said, "I'll be there."

I decided to take the bus to Chicago, then I would rent a car and drive to Green Bay. When I got to Chicago and went to rent an automobile, I was told they would not rent me a car because I did not have a credit card. Even back then that was a problem. So I called my cousin in Milwaukee and asked him, if I could get to Milwaukee, could he drive me to Green Bay. He said sure. I took the bus to Milwaukee and he drove me to Green Bay so I could get to practice on Tuesday.

I was excited about getting there, because the Pittsburgh Steelers in those days were one of three teams you didn't want to play for: the Steelers, the Redskins, and the Bears. They were the cheapest teams in the league. Sonny Parker, the Steelers coach, was from the old school. There was no discipline. Guys like myself and the rookies would work our butts off in practice, and then [veteran] guys like Bobby Layne and Big Daddy Lipscomb just had to sit around and not do anything

Looking back, I had played against the Packers in Milwaukee in '62, and I remember that I had had a fairly good game against them. When I got to the Steelers as a rookie, I weighed only 175 pounds as a running back, and in those days you still had guys playing both offense and defense [in college]. Well, they had all kinds of running backs and so they [the Steelers] made a wide receiver out of me. But the Steelers didn't have a wide receivers coach. You just learned from the films and from talking with your teammates. About three or four games into the season, they picked up Bob Schnelker from the Giants. They kept him for about a month and then let him go. So in '66 when the Packers needed a receiver, I really think Bob Schnelker, who by then was with the Packers, put the good word in for me.

Getting back to Green Bay and my first week of practice there. On Friday, Coach Lombardi called me over and said, "Red, you're a veteran. You probably won't get to play much on offense, but you'll be on special teams and you'll be all right." I got activated right away.

One thing about the Packers: Usually when you go from one team to another in the league, you feel like an outsider with your new team; I never got that feeling with the Packers. All the guys were nice to me. They would tell me things like, "Hey, if you want to get your hair cut, go see Tony the barber," and "If you want to get your car washed, go see this guy." "If you need to get some cleaning done, go to see this cleaners." You know, stuff like that. I didn't have a place to live, and with the season getting ready to start, some players told me about a guy who was getting ready to open some new apartments. He said he would have a place ready in two weeks, so I went to live in a hotel for two weeks while my wife stayed back in South Bend. One time when my youngest boy got really sick, and this was after my wife had joined me in Green Bay, we didn't know any doctors, but someone from the team told us to go see a particular doctor. We were taken care of. I was a teammate right away. I wasn't an outsider. They even gave me a raise when I went to the Packers—they said I wasn't making enough money. It made me feel like I had worked all those years for something worthwhile.

Even though I was on second team, Coach Lombardi made me feel like my job was just as important as Bart Starr's or Ray Nitschke's or Fuzzy Thurston's, which meant that I always had to be paying attention and giving 100 percent just like all the other guys. Number one, they had the discipline; number two, everybody knew his job; and number three, everyone gave 100 percent. They accomplished more in one day of practice than the Pittsburgh Steelers had been able to do in an entire week. Everything was done professionally and everything went real smoothly. Actually, we didn't spend a lot of time out on the practice field. Most of our time was spent in meetings, and Lombardi made everybody feel a genuine part of the team.

He would put the game plan up on the board, and if somebody didn't like the plan or what they were doing, he didn't argue, he would just cross it off and say, "Hey, if we can't run it, we won't run it." With everybody being a part of the game plan and all, when you went into the stadium on Sunday, the Packers felt like they were going to win because we had put the time and effort into it during the week.

There was no guessing about what we were going to do and what we were capable of doing. It was all cut and dried.

I was impressed with Lombardi because it was a business and everybody was part of it. Nobody was left out. You never left a meeting feeling like you weren't wanted. Probably the most influential thing he ever did for me was when he said that there were three things a guy needed to do and that was love his family, love his religion, and love his job. If he did that, he was a success. And to this day, that is one of the ways with which I have always measured myself. My wife and I have been married for thirty-nine years. I worked at Allied Signal for thirty-three years, and my wife and I have been to church every Sunday as practicing Catholics. All of my boys are out of college and have gotten married, and that's something that we had to work for. That lesson he gave in '67 wasn't about football—it was about being a person. Every person who came to Green Bay to play for him he tried to make a complete person. That's how he ran everything. He was like a father to forty-something men.

I remember after winning the Super Bowl that year I was at my station in the locker room and I was crying. He came up to me and said, "What you crying about?" And I said, "You know, this is probably the happiest day in my life because I've never been in this situation before—I've never been with a championship team." And he said, "Red, if you didn't belong here, you wouldn't be here."

When I got released by the Packers in '67, it wasn't a deal where Pat Peppler called me to the office and told me to bring my playbook. I went over to the office and he told me to get into the car, that we were going to go over to the country club. So I went to meet Coach at the country club, and he asked me if I wanted to eat with him, and I said, "No, that's all right." He said, "You know, we're going to go with some younger guys this year and I'm going to have to release you. If I can do anything for you, such as getting you a job to coach or play in the Eastern League, I've got a job for you. If not, if there is anything I can do for you as a reference, give me a call anytime." He took the time to tell me that he was going to make some changes and didn't leave it up to someone else on the staff. That's the way he was. I was just happy to be on that club and being associated with people who were so professional about what they did.

Tex Schramm *on Lombardi, the kindhearted braveheart:*

He was a different person in person from the way you imagined him with his team out on the football field. Vince was a very kindhearted, sweet person, the kind who would do anything for you even though he was a very important, influential man in the National Football League. He never gave you the impression of being a league big shot in our committee meetings or on a personal basis. You talk about a guy that can be dogmatic or whatever you want to call it, he could be, but he was never that way. There was no feeling of animosity or feeling of friction involving the members. And you're talking about three of the most looked-upon people in sports. It was a great committee.

Wellington Mara, *Giants owner and fellow Fordham alum:*

If you said good morning to him in the right way, you could bring tears to his eyes.[6]

Packers wide receiver **Max McGee:**

He's got to be the most egotistical man I ever met. I swear he preached humility to enhance his own ego.[7]

During the 1962 season, Lombardi agreed to coauthor a book, Run to Daylight! to be published by Prentice-Hall as part of a series of sports books featuring successful sports figures teamed with top-notch writers. Lombardi would provide the book's expertise while veteran scribe W. C. Heinz was hired to be the coach's coauthor. Several weeks before the start of training camp in July 1962, Lombardi invited Heinz to stay at the Lombardis' home in Green Bay. After three intense days of pouring out his football knowledge to Heinz, Lombardi figured his work on the book was about over. But Heinz informed the coach otherwise, saying that those three days had produced enough material to fill only one of Heinz's notebooks and part of a second, when in fact he would need about six notebooks of material for a complete book. Needless to say, Lombardi was livid:

Six notebooks? Six notebooks? How am I going to do six notebooks? Six notebooks? I've got paperwork to do at the office! I've got players I haven't signed yet! I've gotta play golf! Once training camp starts, I can't play [golf] again until the end of the season! Six notebooks? How are we ever gonna do six notebooks?[8]

Milwaukee Journal *reporter* **Terry Bledsoe,** *recalling the first time he tried to get some postgame quotes from Lombardi, in 1962:*

I walk into the shower room and here's this short, fat guy toweling himself off. And he sees me and snarls, "Who the hell are you?" He answered a few questions, but it was clear I was on borrowed time, so I got the hell out of there."[9]

Tex Maule, Sports Illustrated *writer:*

Whenever they'd get to a new city, Vinnie would read off the list of bars and restaurants that were off-limits. Well, they'd get to Chicago on a Saturday and of course the list there was a long one. Once Lombardi read what must have been a list of two hundred bars, and when he got through he was furious, just because it had taken so much time to read them. So Max McGee says, "Jeez, Coach, you don't expect me to make all of those places in one night, do you? Next year let's come down on a Friday at least." Vinnie damn near split a gut.[10]

Vince Jr. *talks about his relationship with his dad:*

My dad and I were never that close. We always had disagreements. Oh, we would always hug and give each other a pat on the back. But whenever I came home from college, or even high school, he'd find the dirtiest jobs for me to work at, such as factory construction or whatever. But by the middle of summer he'd ask, "Do you want to go to training camp?" "Hell, yes, I wanted to go," I'd say. "I'll do anything to get out of this lousy job you've got me." And so I'd go off to training camp and be a water boy, ball boy, or that kind of stuff you do. Still, he'd chew me out for something, right in front of the players, because I'd done something like not get the balls out there on time. I'm sure the players saw this and thought to themselves, *Geez, even his kid's not above getting yelled at,* and that probably had something to do with motivating them further.

Vince Jr., a fullback, was a pretty fair football player in his own right, excelling in high school before going on to play college ball at Saint Thomas College in Saint Paul, Minnesota. His father was able to make it to about two or three games a year, such as when the Packers played nearby against the Minnesota Vikings:

After my games he would usually say, at first, that I had played a pretty good game and then he would go into stuff like picking up my feet higher when I ran or something else that I could have done better. But it was a constructive critique, and I took it as such.

As much as Vince Sr. critiqued his son's football abilities, he had very little sympathy for injuries. Vince Jr.:

191

When I was a freshman in college, I hurt my knee right away, even before school had started. Anyway, soon after that the Packers had a game in Minneapolis. I walked into the team hotel on Saturday afternoon limping, and a lot of his players were in the lobby giving me lots of sympathy and all that because again I was doing quite well and we were becoming friends.

After a while I walked up to my dad's suite of rooms, where he gave me a big hug, a big smile, and a "How ya' doin'," all because of my knee. He had the team doctor there with him for the express purpose of looking at my knee. The doctor yanked it this way, he yanked it that way, and then he said, "Well, it's pretty loose but all things considered you can probably get by [if you play] on it. At that point my dad lit into me, just yelling at me and saying, "You're gonna run on it tomorrow! Quit babying it." In the course of a five-minute conversation, he had gone from a hug to where now I had tears running down my face. I was just a little [kid], and he was just whipping me. But, you know, I ran on it the next day, and I started about three weeks later.

In the early sixties Lombardi wrote Run to Daylight! *which became a best-selling primer on the game and added another merit badge to Lombardi's enduring reputation. The inspiration for the book's title?* **Larry Higgins,** *one of Lombardi's former players at both Saints and Fordham, says it was him:*

As Andy Warhol once said, everybody gets his or her fifteen minutes of fame, and this was mine.

It was while we were at Fordham. It was on a Monday following a game against Boston College. In that game, we had died on offense four times inside the twenty-yard line. At that Monday's practice, Lombardi told us we were going to practice plays all week long designed to make us successful in the red zone. So that day we practiced and practiced and practiced my mostly off-tackle plays. Lombardi was running around perfecting the downfield blocking, the line blocking, and all of my fullback plays. Anyway, we practiced until twilight, and it was getting dark on the field.

There was this big, tall hedge about fifteen feet high out there. As the sun was going down, descending behind that hedge, we were running a play in which I ran to the left-hand side, where all I could see were silhouettes. I couldn't see anything. And I would take what we called a stagger step and make a fake, and then I'd turn around and see nothing but silhouettes [of other players]. I couldn't see the hole and would run into my guards, meaning I was screwing up every time I'd run left. But when we ran to the right, even though we had the same silhouettes, the sun was reflecting off one of the white buildings adjacent to the field. And as I took my stagger step and came back toward the hole, I could actually see the hole because of what remaining sunlight there was reflecting off the building. It was daylight. This time, I could see the parting of the silhouettes and could see the hole and run to it. Well, Lombardi was really ticked at one point. He came over, put his head next to mine, and shouted like hell, "What in the world is going on! Every time you run to the left you screw up!" And I said, "Coach, when I run to the right I can see daylight, the reflection of the sun. I could see the light and I'd run to daylight." And Lombardi laughed and said, "Okay, everyone, we're going to run to daylight." And the term "run to daylight" became very familiar.

I never told anyone that story until a few years ago when I told it over dinner and wine to a guy my daughter was dating, a guy who was on the *New York Times* sports staff. He asked me to write it up, which I eventually did. I still get a big kick out of it to this day, thinking, *Hey, Lombardi stole my line!*

*As a former West Point quarterback under Lombardi who went on to a long career in the corporate world of business, **Peter Vann** can stand back and paint a picture from afar of Lombardi, Inc., and how he developed himself over time:*

I think he grew and knew that there was a level that people could really absorb and then beyond that you're trying to force too much into them. Vince started building a foundation on Day One and then the second year he could build on that foundation and the house got bigger. The basement was constructed the first year and then he started to put down the various levels of floors. And you have the second floor, the third floor, the fourth floor. So I think Vince over time learned the big picture. At West Point, he wasn't yet the total epitome of football knowledge, but he gained an awful lot from Colonel Blaik and then he gained from the New York Giants. And he gained a heck of a lot in his first season at Green Bay, too. He got taken to the cleaners a few times, but he was one of those types of guys you'd like to have in a corporation, that just keeps growing and growing and getting stronger and stronger, and ultimately you just turn the corporation over to him.

At West Point you probably wouldn't turn a corporation over to Vince Lombardi. With the Giants, hey, you might turn the first or second shift over to Vince Lombardi. And then the first year at Green Bay is another steppingstone.

Even though nearly a quarter-century had gone by since he had last played for Lombardi at Fordham, **Larry Higgins** *remembers going to a Redskins game in 1969 and from afar picking up, like radar, a familiar loud voice from years gone by.*

Lombardi would scream at us when we played for him. That's one way he motivated us. He had the loudest voice that I have ever heard in my entire life. I mean you couldn't possibly not pay attention to him, because his voice was so hard and he would individually come and put his head right next to your face and holler at you. And I defy anyone to say, "Oh, well, I'm not going to pay attention to him." It was very powerful the way he used to do it. Years later, I got to hear him again after he had gone to the Washington Redskins. You've got to remember, the Redskins were playing in one of those big ol' stadiums made out of cement. I was at a game, seated up in the stands with some friends, when it dawned on me at halftime that I could hear him screaming way down below, through all those layers of cement and even with all the other noise going on at halftime. At first, all I heard was a voice before I realized whose it was. I turned to my friends and told them to shush and listen. "Quiet," I said, "and listen." After a few seconds I asked them if they could hear what I heard, a guy yelling. They said, "Yeah, who is it?" and I said, "Damn, it's Lombardi."

195

Lombardi to Paul Hornung after Hornung had been suspended indefinitely after the 1962 season for gambling on football games, along with Alex Karras of the Detroit Lions:

You stay at the foot of the cross. I don't want to see you go to the racetrack. I don't want to hear about you going to the [Kentucky] Derby. I don't want to hear about you doing anything. Keep your nose clean, and I'll do my best to get you back. But, mister, stay at the foot of the cross.[11]

Chicago Tribune *sportswriter* **Cooper Rollow:**

[Lombardi] was really awful in his treatment of people. We always used to say that Lombardi can get [away] with his high-handed, arrogant tactics as long as he keeps winning, but if he ever starts losing, God help him, he's really going to be in trouble with the media, the fans, the players—with everybody.[12]

Longtime NFL commissioner **Pete Rozelle:**

He was a highly ethical person. He followed the rules. Once, though, he was very upset with the officials, and he followed them into their dressing room after the game telling them what he thought. Well, of course, there is a provision in the league constitution that prohibits a coach from doing this, and when the matter was reported to me I knew I had to do something. In Vinnie's case I thought about what he'd done and the degree of its severity, and I thought about it for a long time. I finally thought that there is a way of disciplining Vinnie that'd be much more effective than saying, You are fined X number of dollars. So I wrote him a letter and the theme of it was that I was amazed and shocked to learn of his actions after the game. I said I was shocked because they came from a man who is so personally dedicated to authority and respect for order. I told him I felt it was totally out of line with what he stood for. In a subsequent phone conversation I discovered the letter had a tremendous impact on him. He felt very sheepish. The letter had hurt him, and it had had its effect. It was far more effective than if I'd fined him $5,000.[13]

Many teams talk about a team concept, but West Point players under Blaik and Lombardi ate, drank, slept, and breathed it, so much so that quarterback **Peter Vann** *never knew he was one of the top-ten-rated Heisman Trophy candidates in 1954, a year after Lombardi left:*

We didn't as a team think very much of records or individual stuff. We were gullible. We played like a team, and that came from Lombardi. Ten years after graduation I had a guy tell me that I had been ninth in the players rating that the Downtown Athletic Club put together. I said, "You're kidding." He said, "No, you call the New York Downtown Athletic Association." I did, and I talked to the secretary who knew my name quite well, and she said, "Oh, I know you, Peter Vann. Let me have you talk to the executive director who was an ardent West Point follower." And they sent me a copy of the Heisman book that goes out every year, and there it is, showing in 1954 that Alan Ameche won it. There under ninth position was Peter Vann, quarterback, West Point. That's sort of symbolic of us as a team not being really interested in anything but excellence, team excellence, not individual shining stars whatsoever. Frankly, that was Lombardi.

You look at the Packers, and I got kind of an interesting insight into those guys, too. In 1960 I got out of the service and joined General Motors in Milwaukee. When Vince's secretary found out I was in Milwaukee, I was invited down every Saturday that the Pack was playing at Milwaukee County Stadium. I would have lunch with the team and then go out to the practice. And there was Bart Starr and Jimmy Ringo and Fuzzy Thurston, and the attitude of that team was very emblematic of the attitude that we had at West Point in our training camp. It was team, team, team, and no big star. Even Hornung and Jimmy Taylor and Max McGee, you know, real big names, they were just people. And it was just kind of interesting that you could see in the Lombardi team structure how things were at West Point.

Sam Huff may have been the only player to have played on two NFL teams that included Lombardi as a coach, without one of those teams being the Green Bay Packers. Huff was a linebacker for the Giants starting in the fifties and in 1969 joined the Redskins as a sort of player-coach under Lombardi:

Lombardi studied the offense, he studied the defense, and he studied the personnel. I never knew General Patton, but I saw the movie and Lombardi was very much like Patton. In fact, you can actually say that a football game is very much like war. You've got to gain ground on the ground and be able to attack through the air, all the while knowing what kind of defense your opponent is throwing at you. People say Patton was a genius in a certain way, and I guess you could say the same thing about Lombardi.

General MacArthur and Colonel Blaik were exactly the kind of people that Lombardi enjoyed being around. Vince always talked about Red Blaik and about his time at Army. That was really his life. There were times I think he thought he had been born again in the sense of being reincarnated, that he had once been a great military guy in another life. At least, that's kind of the opinion he gave when you were around him. I mean, think about it: He was into conditioning, he believed strongly in tactics, and he believed in attacking a team's strength and breaking their wills.

Insurance agent **Jack Koeppler** *was one of Lombardi's good golf buddies, a three-handicapper who enjoyed playing best-ball matches teamed with Lombardi because the coach, who shot in the mid-80s, had a knack for delivering in the clutch, time and again:*

It was amazing how well he could play if I happened to miss a shot. If I was playing well, he would just play along. But if I happened to knock it somewhere not as good as it should be, he could just focus on making that thing do what he wanted it to do. Some guys go the other way. When playing with a low-handicap player, and that guy gets stuck somewhere, they get it stuck worse. Vince may hit only three or four good shots a round, but they were the ones that saved us. Of course, we would win quite a few matches before they started; the other team would be three or four down before they got over the fact that they were playing against Vince Lombardi.[14]

Steve Sabol, *producer for NFL Films, surmised that Lombardi's incredible presence as an authority figure came from his voice:*

It was all the voice. The great leaders in history—Kennedy, Martin Luther King Jr., Roosevelt, Hitler—all had these really unique voices. And Lombardi's voice was so unique, so strident, so resonant, it could cut through anything. He could be on the other side of a room and talking in his regular tone, and everyone would hear him.[15]

*Vince Lombardi was not an outdoors guy—outdoors in the sense of being at home with a deer-hunting rifle or fishing rod in his hands. So it was only natural that he was out of his element one time when he and two other friends at West Point took their sons—**Vince Jr.** included—on a camping trip up in Quebec. It was supposed to be a vacation, or at least a getaway for the guys, but Vince Sr. couldn't get back to the football field quick enough. Vince Jr. recalls:*

There weren't any roads around. We took the last road, and when that road ended we put the canoes in the water. And my dad was not an outdoors guy. I mean, he could handle it, but it was something we did that we were doing together and not something he *wanted* to do.

In the canoes we were switching off with the boys, in that each boy would go with one of the other two men. Being youngsters, we were very light, and it was important to know how to position ourselves in the canoe. At one point in the river we entered some eddies and a whirlpool, and Dad couldn't handle it. He got caught going around and around and around and couldn't get the canoe to go anywhere because the front of the canoe was almost pointing straight up into the air. Somebody had to go over there and put somebody heavier in the front of the canoe just to get the front down so we could get under way again. It was a good time, but I don't recall ever doing that again.

AP/WIDE WORLD PHOTOS

Vincent T. Lombardi

6

LOMBARDI SPEAKS OUT

He wasn't a media darling. He didn't say much; he revealed practically nothing. Nor was he particularly photogenic. Reporters didn't have much of an ally in Lombardi, and he couldn't have cared less. He would give an honest, albeit unrevealing answer when asked a question, as long as it was a question that showed at least a reasonable amount of football know-how on the part of the inquisitor. Lombardi didn't suffer fools gladly or without the occasional verbal spat. Under the glare of today's omnipresent cameras, intrusive microphones, and irreverent Dennis Millers, who knows how Lombardi would have reacted? Or even if he would have bothered with the NFL.

But if Lombardi wasn't a memorable interview, he still was a man of profound words. Whether or not he actually coined the phrase "Winning isn't everything; it's the only thing," he was the first coach to become a one-man cottage industry of motivational sayings and inspirational jargon. Some of it was his own material; some was borrowed, sometimes even modified a bit and called his own. Which is okay because he had a context into which he could fit anything he said. Lombardi was very well read, too, perhaps not in the sense of being an authentic Renaissance man, but heck, the guy could translate Greek and Latin.

Give the coach a pen and paper or an attentive audience of business executives, and he could crank out memorable sayings and dazzling anecdotes, all designed to tickle an ear while making a point. He could sweet-talk a growling Ray Nitschke when the situation called for it, and he could yell fear straight into the heart of an underperforming slacker. An emotional man, he would occasionally let his guard down and his refreshing candor would come pouring out, whether it was singing the praises of someone who had knocked himself silly for the good of the team or ripping his star players when he knew it was the entire team that needed a swift kick before playing a "meaningless" opponent. Lombardi had a way with words, and he was a man of his word.

On how football is part of the American fabric:

I've been in football all my life, and I don't know whether I'm particularly qualified to be a part of anything else, except I consider it a great game, a game of many assets, by the way, and I think a symbol of what this country's best attributes are: courage and stamina and a coordinated efficiency or teamwork.[1]

On being able to enjoy the drive into work on Sunday for that day's game:

Six days a week this traffic light is the one thing that invades my consciousness as I drive to work, that consistently interrupts that single purpose of winning next Sunday's game. By Saturday, if we have not solved the problems that started accumulating on Monday, it is too late to worry about it, and so driving into town I am aware of the scenes around me for the first time in a week.[2]

On the close-knit aspect of being a team:

There's a great closeness on a football team, you know—a rapport between the men and the coach that's like no other sport. It's a binding together, a knitting together. For me, it's like fathers and sons, and that's what I missed. I missed players coming up to me and saying, "Coach, I need some help because my baby's sick." Or, "Mr. Lombardi, I want to talk with you about trouble I'm having with my wife." That's what I missed most. The closeness.[3]

On playing hurt:

Forget about that cracked rib. You don't even need it.[4]
You can't hurt a charley horse.[5]

On his being relatively short:

I'm no Napoleon, whatever the writers think. You know, he used to have his colonels, or whatever you call them, a couple of inches shorter than him to make him seem bigger. . . . With me, the bigger those colonels are, the better.[6]

On the value of simplicity:

I have been called a tyrant, but I have also been called the coach of the simplest system in football, and I suppose there is some truth in both of those. The perfect name for the perfect coach would be Simple Simon Legree.[7]

On his faith walk with God:

When we place our dependence in God, we are unencumbered, and we have no worry. In fact, we may even be reckless, insofar as our part in the production is concerned. This confidence, this sureness of action, is both contagious and an aid to the perfect action. The rest is in the hands of God—and this is the same God, gentlemen, who has won all His battles up to now.[8]

On faith and football:

Never pray for victory. Pray for the will of God.[9]

206

On telling his Saint Cecilia's football players how to think:

I'll do all the thinking. Just do exactly as I tell you. I'll take the responsibility. Don't improvise![10]

On his temper:

Like my father before me, I have a violent temper with which I have been struggling all my life.[11]

Lombardi in a February 1967 speech he gave in New York to a meeting of more than a thousand corporate executives:

[Football] is a symbol, I think, of what this country's best attributes are; namely, courage, stamina, and coordinated efficiency. It is a Spartan game, and I mean by that, it requires Spartanlike qualities in order to play it, and I am speaking of the Spartan qualities of sacrifice and self-denial rather than that other Spartan quality of leaving the weak to die.[12]

Lombardi on leadership, from the same speech in New York:

The leader must be willing to use [leadership]. His leadership is then based on truth and character. There must be truth in the purpose and willpower in the character. Leadership rests not only upon ability but upon commitment and upon loyalty and upon pride and upon followers. . . . A leader is composed of not just one quality but a blend of many, and each must develop their own particular combination to their own personality. Leaders are made; they are not born. They are made by hard effort, which is the price which all of us must pay to achieve any goal that is worthwhile.[13]

On the dynamics and value of a meeting:

A meeting is only a means of communication. Its purpose should be to produce a change in procedure. This procedure could be in knowledge, attitude, behavior, or skill. In our meetings, management gives information, it collects information, it pools information, and it discusses the best way to approach the problem. We have one hard and fast rule: Once the group is agreed upon the method, there is no deviation until the group agrees to the change.[14]

On organizational achievement:

The achievements of an organization are the results of the combined efforts of each individual.[15]

On his awkward first meeting of 1959 draftee Billy Butler, who showed up at Packers camp somewhat smaller even than the five-foot-ten, 180 pounds listed on his program from college:

What the hell are you doing here? This line isn't for kids![16]

On his being hired by the Packers before the 1959 season:

I have been hired to do a job without interference, and I don't expect to have any. If you don't like me . . .[17]

On his being hired in 1959 by the Packers, speaking at his introductory press conference:

I have never been associated with a loser, and I don't expect to be now.[18]

On explaining his uncharacteristic graciousness during an interview with a reporter one spring day:

This is March. I don't have to start worrying until June. This is my free time.[19]

On his personality:

I'm not an overly modest man. Sure, I'm humble, but I've never been overly modest. What happened [at Green Bay] isn't so hard to explain. A good coach is a good coach, right? If you take all twenty-six coaches in pro football and look at their football knowledge, you'd find there's almost no difference. So if the knowledge isn't different, what's different? The coach's personality. See? Now, how am I supposed to explain my own personality? What am I supposed to say? That I'm a great leader? A mental powerhouse? That I've got charisma?[20]

On his trying to make up with then-fiancée and future wife Marie Planitz after an argument that broke off their engagement, his feelings written in a note that he left for her:

Darling Rie, I love you so much, Rie. I'm sorry about last night. I'm with you 100 percent. . . . Have been here since 10:00 this morning. Alone since 11:30 A.M.—it is now about 1:00. Intend to leave soon. I even brought up some buns this A.M.— thought maybe you and I could have some coffee and—Sorry to have missed you, Honey. I love you with all my heart. I mean that. Sincerely, Vincent.[21]

On his marriage:

The great thing about Marie is that she knocks me down when I'm up, and she picks me up when I'm down.[22]

On assessing his Packers in the middle of a sloppy practice before they were to play the Los Angeles Rams in a late-season game in 1966 with a playoff berth already wrapped up:

You fellows don't have any pride. All you have is shame. You're a disgrace to the National Football League. I don't know who you guys think you are. If the Rams beat you, you'll never come back. You fellows are supposed to be a championship team, but you must have been lucky to get where you are. Let's get back at it and do it right. [The Packers won, 27-23.][23]

On the prospects of his running for political office after being approached to consider running for the U.S. Senate or governorship of Wisconsin:

I gave it some thought. I wasn't sure my nature was right for it. You know, I'm pretty sensitive to what they say about me in the sports pages. I wasn't sure I could take the beating you get in public life. At the same time, I liked to think I could make a contribution to people. And then I was asked to go with a lot of big corporations, and that tempted me, too. You like to think you can rise to a new challenge. But I wasn't sure about those things.[24]

On the importance of having good offensive guards on your team:

It's a funny thing in football that when a team has a weakness it always stays with them. There have been NFL teams that could have been champions except that they lacked good offensive guards. They trade for them and they draft them, but year after year guards are always their weakness. And year after year they're losers.[25]

On his decision to forgo a field goal and instead go for the touchdown with the Packers trailing Dallas 17-14 with seconds remaining and the ball on the Cowboys' one-yard line:

I didn't figure those fans in the stands wanted to sit through a sudden death. You can't say I'm without compassion, although I've been accused of it.[26]

On his sideline instructions to quarterback Bart Starr for the pivotal third-down, goal-line play against the Dallas Cowboys in the waning moments of the 1967 Ice Bowl, officially known as the NFL Championship Game:

Run it! And let's get the hell out of here.[27]

On race:

If you're black or white, you're a part of the family. We make no issue over a man's color. I just won't tolerate anybody in this organization, coach or player, making it an issue. We respect every man's dignity, black or white. I won't stand for any movements or groups on our ball club. It comes down to a question of love. . . . You just have to love your fellow man, and it doesn't matter whether he is black or white. If anything is bothering any of our players—black and white alike—we settle whatever it is right away.[28]

On one of what he saw as several reasons for his not getting a head-coaching job beyond high school earlier than he did:

I know I lost some jobs because of my Italian heritage.[29]

On his use of the word hate *in motivating his team to play an opponent:*

I won't renege on that word. I'll stand by it. When I say "hate," I don't mean I wish anybody any physical harm. Do I mean I want him to run out on the field and hit a man, or kick him, or fall on top of him and pummel him? No. I wouldn't do that. But I do have to build up an emotion before a game to do a good job. If I go out there feeling just fine about everything and everybody, I'm not going to do the job I should do.[30]

On the anxiety of winning a game by too many points:

I have been asleep for three hours and, suddenly, I am awake. I am awake, and that's the trouble with this game. Just twelve hours ago I walked off that field, and we had beaten the Bears, 49 to 0. Now I should be sleeping the satisfied sleep of the contented, but I am lying here awake, wide awake, seeing myself walking across that field, seeing myself searching in the crowd for George Halas but really hoping that I would not find him.

All week long there builds up inside of you a competitive animosity toward that other man, that counterpart across the field. All week long he is the symbol, the epitome, of what you must defeat and then, when it is over, when you have looked up to that man for as long as I have looked up to George Halas, you cannot help but be disturbed by a score like this. You know he brought a team in here hurt by key injuries and that this was just one of those days, but you can't apologize. You can't apologize for a score. It is up there on that board and nothing can change it now. I can just hope, lying here awake in the middle of the night, that after all those years he has had in this league —and he has had forty-two of them—these things no longer affect him as they still affect me. I can just hope that I am making more of this than he is, and now I see myself, unable to find him in the crowd and walking up that ramp and into our dressing room, now searching instead for something that will bring my own team back to earth.[31]

On his being a hard-driving coach:

It's no damn fun being hard. I've been doing this for years and years and years. It's never been great fun. You have to drive yourself constantly. I don't enjoy it. It takes a hell of a lot out of me. And, Christ, you get kind of embarrassed with yourself sometimes. You berate somebody, and you feel disgusted with yourself for doing it, for being in a job where you have to. Fortunately, I don't remember.[32]

On mental toughness:

I'm in the line of traffic now, and I guess what it comes down to is that success demands singleness of purpose. In this game we're always looking for catch-phrases, especially with a connotation of masculinity, so I call it mental toughness. They have written about the mental toughness with which I supposedly have instilled this team and, when they ask me what it is, I have difficulty explaining it. I think it is single-ness of purpose and, once you have agreed upon the price that you and your family must pay for success, it enables you to forget that price.[33]

On how he was able to learn so much about upcoming opponents thanks to his acquired taste for dissecting game film at West Point:

It's surprising how many players tipped themselves off by the position of their feet, the angle of their body. You could tell whether it was a wedge play, pass play, dive play, sweep. You see whether a lineman can be had to the inside. You make notes on paper and put books together on the forma-tions and their personnel.[34]

On the complexity of the game:

I do not believe this game is as complex as many people think it is and as some try to make it. At the same time I don't think it is as simple as it was twenty years ago. We try to make it as uncomplicated as we can, because I believe that if you block and tackle better than the other team and the breaks are even, you're going to win, but we can't make it quite as simple as playground tag.[35]

On his frustration at age forty-three in 1956 about still not getting a head-coaching job at the major college or professional level soon after losing out at Penn and Washington:

I'm wondering whether the right head-coaching job ever will open up for me. I know I can coach, but the right people never seem to know it.[36]

On his final instructions to his Packers office staff before leaving on a Caribbean vacation following the 1960 season that had culminated in an NFL Championship Game loss to the Philadelphia Eagles, just two years removed from the Packers' 1-10-1 season prior to Lombardi's arrival:

While I'm gone, I don't want any slovenly work around here. Do what you're supposed to do![37]

On the first day of training camp in 1961:

I'm scared.[38]

On the length of practices:

I am not for long practice sessions, but I am for an hour or an hour and a half that is meticulously organized and intense, and this, too, is something that I got from Earl Blaik and brought away from West Point. We would arrive at that office every morning at eight and by the time we walked out onto the practice field that afternoon we would have worked out every phase and every time schedule for everything. Blaik allowed no papers on the field, so I had to have every assignment for every lineman on every play because every bit of offense and defense was given on the field, and that first spring I couldn't comprehend how you could get it all across to those cadets without a meeting.[39]

On the meaning of love:

Love is the respect for the dignity of an individual—love is charity. The love I speak of is not detraction. A man who belittles another—who is not charitable to another, who has no respect for the dignity of his fellow man, who is not loyal, who speaks ill of another—is not a leader and does not belong in the top-management echelon.[40]

On his emotional nature:

Hell, I'm an emotional man. I cry. I cried when we won the Super Bowl, and I cried when I left Green Bay. I'm not ashamed of crying.[41]

On teaching vs. coaching:

They call it coaching, but it is teaching. You do not just tell them it is so, but you show them the reasons why it is so and you repeat until they are convinced, until they know.[42]

On leadership amid the erosion of societal values:

Maybe we have so long ridiculed authority in the family, discipline in education, decency in conduct, and law in the state, that our freedom has brought us close to chaos. This could be because our leaders no longer understand the relationship between themselves and the people; that is, the people want to be independent and dependent, all at the same time, to assert themselves and at the same time be told what to do.[43]

On dealing with rookies in summer camp:

It is amazing how on that first day one or two impress you with the grace with which they move. Even before some of them put on a uniform you get that feeling from them. And then there's another one and you'll wonder why you ever brought him into camp. You have two reactions. First you feel an urge to work just on that good one, to see how perfect you can make him. But then you realize, you must work on the others, too, in order to make a team, and so you spend most of the time you can give—and it's never enough—with the ones who lack natural ability, but whom you need.[44]

On his thumbnail assessment of Packers quarterback Bart Starr:

Tense by nature, because he's a perfectionist. I've never seen him display emotion outside of nervousness. Modest. Tends to be self-effacing, which is usually a sign of lack of ego. You never hear him in the locker room telling "I" stories. He calls me "sir." Seems shy, but he's not. He's just a gentleman. You don't criticize him in front of others.[45]

On Paul Hornung:

Can take criticism in public or anywhere. You have to whip him a little. He had a hell-with-you attitude, a defensive perimeter he built around himself when he didn't start out well here. As soon as he had success, he changed. He's still exuberant, likes to play around, but serious on the field.[46]

On Willie Davis:

Very excitable under game conditions. A worrier. Before a game he's got that worried look, so I try to bolster his confidence. He's not worried about the team losing—he's got confidence in the team—but he's worried about how Willie Davis will perform. . . . Fine brain, too.[47]

On tough-guy player Ray Nitschke:

Nitschke is the rowdy of this team and the whipping boy because he needs it and he can take it. He has the proper temperament for a middle linebacker, but maybe too much of it. He is a big, 6-foot-3, 235-pound, rough, belligerent, fun-loving guy with a heart as big as all outdoors, but he's been a problem to coach. When you chew him out he's like a child. He's repentant and never gives you an argument, but then he turns around and does the same thing over again, and one of the best things that ever happened for Nitschke and this ball club is his marriage. It has settled him down. Criticism still rolls off him until you wonder if it helps him at all.[48]

On tight end Marv Fleming's propensity for missing assignments:

Look at you, stupid, you big jerk. You don't have the mental capacity to retain anything for twenty-four hours.[49]

On reacting to different situations:

There is a time when violent reactions are in order. And there are times when purring like a pussycat and bestowing thanks and gratitude are equally desirable. Each of us must learn when the time fits the response and must tailor our action or reaction to each situation.[50]

On trying to get to sleep at night:

The others have gone to bed, but there is no point in my trying to sleep, so I'm watching an old movie on television. Douglas Fairbanks, Jr. is the African white hunter who has hired out to the German baron with the beautiful young wife—and the trouble with me is my ego just can't accept loss. I suppose if I were more perfectly adjusted I could toss off defeat but my name is on this ball club. Thirty-six men publicly reflect me and reflect on me, and it's a matter of my pride.

The German baron wounds a leopard but refuses to track him into the bush. A native bearer is killed by the animal because of the baron's cowardice—and I wonder sometimes if perhaps I transmit to my team the anxiety I feel going into a game.[51]

On his disappointment, as a player, following Fordham's 7-7 tie with Georgia in 1936, ending the Rams' bid for a perfect season and marking the beginning of the end of their chances for playing in the Rose Bowl:

Some of our better players . . . behaved as if we had already finished the season undefeated and had received and accepted the bid to the Rose Bowl we all wanted so badly.[52]

On his reaction to kick returner Travis Williams's fumble moments after paying a compliment to Williams:

Should have kept my big mouth shut.[53]

On getting his players up for next week's game, week after week:

I've got to make them believers, I'm thinking, and then the problem all week will be to get them up again, all of them, for next Sunday. After this, how will I ever get them up again for next Sunday?

That's what I'm thinking now, turning off Oneida Avenue in the traffic. Then for the first time I feel the fatigue coming, the tiredness coming all over me.[54]

On explaining his decision to leave the Packers for good following his one season as only general manager to resume his dual role of head coach and general manager, this time with the Washington Redskins:

I need a challenge and I have found the satisfaction of a challenge is not in maintaining a position but rather in attaining it. I can no more walk away from this challenge than I could have walked away from the one ten years ago. I am the same man today I was ten years ago.[55]

On winning the battle the right way:

No leader, however great, can long continue unless he wins battles. The battle decides all. How does one achieve success in battle? I believe it is essential to understand that battles are won primarily in the hearts of men. Men respond to leadership in a most remarkable way, and once you have won his heart, he will follow you anywhere. Leadership is based on a spiritual quality, the power to inspire, the power to inspire others to follow. This spiritual quality may be for good or for evil. In many cases in the past, this quality has been devoted toward personal ends and was partly or wholly evil. Leadership which is evil, while it may temporarily succeed, always carries within itself the seeds of its own destruction.[56]

On his respect for success:

It's hard to have patience with a society that has sympathy only for the underprivileged. We must have sympathy for the doer, too. We speak of freedom. Sometimes I think we confuse it with license.

Everything is done to strengthen the rights of the individual at the expense of responsibility to the church, state, and authority. We are in the midst of a rebellion, a struggle for the hearts and souls and minds of all of us.

We must help the underprivileged, certainly. But let us also respect success.[57]

On opening a press conference one time:

All right, gentlemen, shall we arrange all of the stupid questions in any priority, or shall we take them all together?[58]

On the life values offered by golf:

I liken it to football because it makes many of the same demands football does. For example, it takes courage—it takes a lot of guts to play golf. And it takes a lot of stamina. It also takes coordinated efficiency—and you must be dedicated to win. . . . If you have sons and if you want them to grow up to be men, have them play the game of golf.[59]

On his general assessment of the Redskins' potential soon after he took over as coach in 1969:

Well, the feeling of being a winner is not in evidence here. Not yet, anyhow. Everybody wants to win, but doing it—. [Sonny] Jurgensen wants to be a winner, but he's never been with a winning club, and it's very difficult for him to suddenly just become one. You've got to be a winner to be a winner, and that's true of Sonny and everybody else on this team.[60]

On facing the Giants for the first time after taking over the Redskins:

One game does not a season make. I would like to say we're all set to go, but it is going to be a long hard pull. Games with the Giants have always been hammer-and-tongs. It will be a ding-dong battle here Sunday.[61]

On one of his fears as he lay dying in Georgetown University Hospital in 1970:

I'm not afraid to die, but there's so much more yet to be done in the world.[62]

APPENDIX

Lombardi's Game-by-Game
NFL Coaching Record

NOTES

INDEX

APPENDIX

Lombardi's Game-by-Game NFL Coaching Record

1959

GREEN BAY PACKERS
(7-5-0)
Tie for Third, Western Conference

DATE	OPPONENT	PLACE	RESULT	POINTS FOR	POINTS ALLOWED
9/27	Chicago Bears	Green Bay	W	9	6
10/4	Detroit Lions	Green Bay	W	28	10
10/11	San Francisco 49ers	Green Bay	W	21	20
10/18	Los Angeles Rams	Milwaukee	L	6	45
10/25	Baltimore Colts	Away	L	21	38
11/1	New York Giants	Away	L	3	20
11/8	Chicago Bears	Away	L	17	28
11/15	Baltimore Colts	Milwaukee	L	24	28
11/22	Washington Redskins	Green Bay	W	21	0
11/26	Detroit Lions	Away	W	24	17
12/6	Los Angeles Rams	Away	W	38	20
12/13	San Francisco 49ers	Away	W	36	14

Home record: 4-2   Away: 3-3   Points for: 248   Points allowed: 246

1960

GREEN BAY PACKERS
(8-4-0)
First, Western Conference

DATE	OPPONENT	PLACE	RESULT	POINTS FOR	POINTS ALLOWED
9/25	Chicago Bears	Green Bay	L	14	17
10/2	Detroit Lions	Green Bay	W	28	9
10/9	Baltimore Colts	Green Bay	W	35	21
10/23	San Francisco 49ers	Milwaukee	W	41	14
10/30	Pittsburgh Steelers	Away	W	19	13
11/6	Baltimore Colts	Away	L	24	38
11/13	Dallas Cowboys	Green Bay	W	41	7
11/20	Los Angeles Rams	Milwaukee	L	31	33
11/24	Detroit Lions	Away	L	10	23
12/4	Chicago Bears	Away	W	41	13
12/10	San Francisco 49ers	Away	W	13	0
12/17	Los Angeles Rams	Away	W	35	21

Home record: 4-2   Away: 4-2   Points for: 332   Points allowed: 209

NFL CHAMPIONSHIP:

12/26	Philadelphia Eagles	Away	L	13	17

1961

GREEN BAY PACKERS
(11-3-0)
First, Western Conference

DATE	OPPONENT	PLACE	RESULT	POINTS FOR	POINTS ALLOWED
9/17	Detroit Lions	Milwaukee	L	13	17
9/24	San Francisco 49ers	Green Bay	W	30	10
10/1	Chicago Bears	Green Bay	W	24	0
10/8	Baltimore Colts	Green Bay	W	45	7
10/15	Cleveland Browns	Away	W	49	17
10/22	Minnesota Vikings	Away	W	33	7
10/29	Minnesota Vikings	Milwaukee	W	28	10
11/5	Baltimore Colts	Away	L	21	45
11/12	Chicago Bears	Away	W	31	28
11/19	Los Angeles Rams	Green Bay	W	35	17
11/23	Detroit Lions	Away	W	17	9
12/3	New York Giants	Milwaukee	W	20	17
12/10	San Francisco 49ers	Away	L	21	22
12/17	Los Angeles Rams	Away	W	24	17

Home record: 6-1   Away: 5-2   Points for: 391   Points allowed: 223

NFL CHAMPIONSHIP:

12/31	New York Giants	Green Bay	W	37	0

1962

GREEN BAY PACKERS
(13-1-0)
First, Western Conference

DATE	OPPONENT	PLACE	RESULT	POINTS FOR	POINTS ALLOWED
9/16	Minnesota Vikings	Green Bay	W	34	7
9/23	Saint Louis Cardinals	Milwaukee	W	17	0
9/30	Chicago Bears	Green Bay	W	49	0
10/7	Detroit Lions	Green Bay	W	9	7
10/14	Minnesota Vikings	Away	W	48	21
10/21	San Francisco 49ers	Milwaukee	W	31	13
10/28	Baltimore Colts	Away	W	17	6
11/4	Chicago Bears	Away	W	38	7
11/11	Philadelphia Eagles	Away	W	49	0
11/18	Baltimore Colts	Green Bay	W	17	13
11/22	Detroit Lions	Away	L	14	26
12/2	Los Angeles Rams	Milwaukee	W	41	10
12/9	San Francisco 49ers	Away	W	31	21
12/16	Los Angeles Rams	Away	W	20	17

Home record: 7-0   Away: 6-1   Points for: 415   Points allowed: 148

NFL CHAMPIONSHIP:

12/30	New York Giants	Away	W	16	7

1963

GREEN BAY PACKERS
(11-2-1)
Second, Western Conference

DATE	OPPONENT	PLACE	RESULT	POINTS FOR	POINTS ALLOWED
9/15	Chicago Bears	Green Bay	L	3	10
9/22	Detroit Lions	Milwaukee	W	31	10
9/29	Baltimore Colts	Green Bay	W	31	20
10/6	Los Angeles Rams	Green Bay	W	42	10
10/13	Minnesota Vikings	Away	W	37	28
10/20	Saint Louis Cardinals	Away	W	30	7
10/27	Baltimore Colts	Away	W	34	20
11/3	Pittsburgh Steelers	Milwaukee	W	33	14
11/10	Minnesota Vikings	Green Bay	W	28	7
11/17	Chicago Bears	Away	L	7	26
11/24	San Francisco 49ers	Milwaukee	W	28	10
11/28	Detroit Lions	Away	Tie	13	13
12/7	Los Angeles Rams	Away	W	31	14
12/14	San Francisco 49ers	Away	W	21	17

Home record: 6-1   Away: 5-1-1   Points for: 369   Points allowed: 206

PLAYOFF BOWL:

1/5	Cleveland Browns	Miami	W	40	23

1964

GREEN BAY PACKERS
(8-5-1)
Tie for Second, Western Conference

DATE	OPPONENT	PLACE	RESULT	POINTS FOR	POINTS ALLOWED
9/13	Chicago Bears	Green Bay	W	23	12
9/20	Baltimore Colts	Green Bay	L	20	21
9/28	Detroit Lions	Away	W	14	10
10/4	Minnesota Vikings	Green Bay	L	23	24
10/11	San Francisco 49ers	Milwaukee	W	24	14
10/18	Baltimore Colts	Away	L	21	24
10/25	Los Angeles Rams	Milwaukee	L	17	27
11/1	Minnesota Vikings	Away	W	42	13
11/8	Detroit Lions	Green Bay	W	30	7
11/15	San Francisco 49ers	Away	L	14	24
11/22	Cleveland Browns	Milwaukee	W	28	21
11/29	Dallas Cowboys	Away	W	45	21
12/5	Chicago Bears	Away	W	17	3
12/13	Los Angeles Rams	Away	Tie	24	24

Home record: 4-3   Away: 4-2-1   Points for: 342   Points allowed: 245

PLAYOFF BOWL:

1/3	Saint Louis Cardinals	Miami	L	17	24

1965

GREEN BAY PACKERS
(10-3-1)
Tie for First, Western Conference

DATE	OPPONENT	PLACE	RESULT	POINTS FOR	POINTS ALLOWED
9/19	Pittsburgh Steelers	Away	W	41	9
9/26	Baltimore Colts	Milwaukee	W	20	17
10/3	Chicago Bears	Green Bay	W	23	14
10/10	San Francisco 49ers	Green Bay	W	27	10
10/17	Detroit Lions	Away	W	31	21
10/24	Dallas Cowboys	Milwaukee	W	13	3
10/31	Chicago Bears	Away	L	10	31
11/7	Detroit Lions	Green Bay	L	7	12
11/14	Los Angeles Rams	Milwaukee	W	6	3
11/21	Minnesota Vikings	Away	W	38	13
11/28	Los Angeles Rams	Away	L	10	21
12/5	Minnesota Vikings	Green Bay	W	24	19
12/12	Baltimore Colts	Away	W	42	27
12/19	San Francisco 49ers	Away	Tie	24	24

Home record: 6-1   Away: 4-2-1   Points for: 316   Points allowed: 224

WESTERN CONFERENCE CHAMPIONSHIP:

12/26	Baltimore Colts	Green Bay	W	13	10

NFL CHAMPIONSHIP:

1/2	Cleveland Browns	Green Bay	W	23	12

1966

GREEN BAY PACKERS
(12-2-0)
First, Western Conference

DATE	OPPONENT	PLACE	RESULT	POINTS FOR	POINTS ALLOWED
9/10	Baltimore Colts	Milwaukee	W	24	3
9/18	Cleveland Browns	Away	W	21	20
9/25	Los Angeles Rams	Green Bay	W	24	13
10/2	Detroit Lions	Green Bay	W	23	14
10/9	San Francisco 49ers	Away	L	20	21
10/16	Chicago Bears	Away	W	17	0
10/23	Atlanta Falcons	Milwaukee	W	56	3
10/30	Detroit Lions	Away	W	31	7
11/6	Minnesota Vikings	Green Bay	L	17	20
11/20	Chicago Bears	Green Bay	W	13	6
11/27	Minnesota Vikings	Away	W	28	16
12/4	San Francisco 49ers	Milwaukee	W	20	7
12/10	Baltimore Colts	Away	W	14	10
12/18	Los Angeles Rams	Away	W	27	23

Home record: 6-1   Away: 6-1   Points for: 335   Points allowed: 163

NFL CHAMPIONSHIP:

1/1	Dallas Cowboys	Away	W	34	27

SUPER BOWL I:

1/15	Kansas City Chiefs	Los Angeles	W	35	10

1967

GREEN BAY PACKERS
(9-4-1)
First, NFL Central

DATE	OPPONENT	PLACE	RESULT	POINTS FOR	POINTS ALLOWED
9/17	Detroit Lions	Green Bay	Tie	17	17
9/24	Chicago Bears	Green Bay	W	13	10
10/1	Atlanta Falcons	Milwaukee	W	23	0
10/8	Detroit Lions	Away	W	27	17
10/15	Minnesota Vikings	Milwaukee	L	7	10
10/22	New York Giants	Away	W	48	21
10/30	Saint Louis Cardinals	Away	W	31	23
11/5	Baltimore Colts	Away	L	10	13
11/12	Cleveland Browns	Milwaukee	W	55	7
11/19	San Francisco 49ers	Green Bay	W	13	0
11/26	Chicago Bears	Away	W	17	13
12/3	Minnesota Vikings	Away	W	30	27
12/9	Los Angeles Rams	Away	L	24	27
12/17	Pittsburgh Steelers	Green Bay	L	17	24

Home record: 4-2-1   Away: 5-2   Points for: 332   Points allowed: 209

WESTERN CONFERENCE CHAMPIONSHIP:

12/23	Los Angeles Rams	Milwaukee	W	28	7

NFL CHAMPIONSHIP:

12/31	Dallas Cowboys	Green Bay	W	21	17

SUPER BOWL II:

1/14	Oakland Raiders	Miami	W	33	14

1969

WASHINGTON REDSKINS, 7-5-2
Second, NFL Capital Division

DATE	OPPONENT	PLACE	RESULT	POINTS FOR	POINTS ALLOWED
9/21	New Orleans Saints	Away	W	26	20
9/28	Cleveland Browns	Away	L	23	27
10/5	San Francisco 49ers	Away	Tie	17	17
10/12	Saint Louis Cardinals	Home	W	33	17
10/19	New York Giants	Home	W	20	14
10/26	Pittsburgh Steelers	Away	W	14	7
10/2	Baltimore Colts	Away	L	17	41
11/9	Philadelphia Eagles	Home	Tie	28	28
11/16	Dallas Cowboys	Home	L	28	41
11/23	Atlanta Falcons	Home	W	27	20
11/30	Los Angeles Rams	Home	L	13	24
12/7	Philadelphia Eagles	Away	W	34	29
12/14	New Orleans Saints	Home	W	17	14
12/21	Dallas Cowboys	Away	L	10	20

Home record: 4-2-1   Away: 3-3-1   Points for: 307   Points allowed: 319

NOTES

Chapter 1: Teacher, Teacher

1. John Wiebusch, ed., *Lombardi* (Chicago: Triumph Books, 1997), 68.
2. Ibid., 67.
3. Ibid.
4. Ibid.
5. Michael O'Brien, *Vince: A Personal Biography of Vince Lombardi* (New York: Morrow, 1987), 87.
6. Ibid., 209.

Chapter 2: West Point

1. David Maraniss, *When Pride Still Mattered: A Life of Vince Lombardi* (New York: Simon and Schuster, 1999), 100.
2. Bob Carroll, *When the Grass Was Real* (New York: Simon and Schuster, 1993), 96–97.
3. Ibid., 97.
4. Maraniss, *When Pride Still Mattered*, 102.
5. Wiebusch, *Lombardi*, 69.

Chapter 3: Land of the Giants

1. O'Brien, *Vince*, 110.
2. Wiebusch, *Lombardi*, 71.
3. Ibid.
4. Maraniss, *When Pride Still Mattered*, 161.
5. Jennifer Briggs, comp., *Strive to Excel: The Will and Wisdom of Vince Lombardi* (Nashville, Tenn.: Rutledge Hill Press, 1997), 44.
6. Frank Gifford, *Gifford on Courage* (New York: Evans, 1976), quoted in O'Brien, 121.

7. Ibid , 122.

8. Wiebusch, *Lombardi*, 70–71.

9. Ibid., 71–72.

10. Ibid., 73.

11. Maraniss, *When Pride Still Mattered*, 201.

12. Wiebusch, *Lombardi*, 78.

Chapter 4: Green Bay and Beyond

1. Wiebusch, *Lombardi*, 83.

2. Maraniss, *When Pride Still Mattered*, 208.

3. O'Brien, *Vince*, 143.

4. Tom Dowling, *Coach: A Season with Lombardi* (New York: Norton, 1970), 17.

5. Ibid., 27.

6. Ibid., 21.

7. Carroll, *When the Grass Was Real*, 58.

8. Wiebusch, *Lombardi*, 39.

9. Carroll, *When the Grass Was Real*, 166.

10. Maraniss, *When Pride Still Mattered*, 374.

11. Wiebusch, *Lombardi*, 84.

12. Bart Starr, *Starr: My Life in Football* (New York: Morrow, 1987), quoted in Briggs, *Strive to Excel*, 15.

13. Briggs, *Strive to Excel*, 39.

14. Wiebusch, *Lombardi*, 45.

15. O'Brien, *Vince*, 193.

16. Ibid., 243.

17. Ibid., 242–43.

18. Briggs, *Strive to Excel*, 73.

19. Ibid., 130–31.

20. Ibid., 72.

21. O'Brien, *Vince*, 248.

22. Jerry Kramer, *Instant Replay: The Green Bay Diary of Jerry Kramer* (New York: Signet, 1969), 49.

23. Ibid., 121.

24. Ibid., 43.

25. Ibid., 20–21.

26. Maraniss, *When Pride Still Mattered*, 495.

27. Dowling, *Coach*, 213–14.

28. Wiebusch, *Lombardi*, 54.

29. Carroll, *When the Grass Was Real*, 196.

30. Briggs, *Strive to Excel*, 131–32.

31. Ibid., 43.

32. Wiebusch, *Lombardi*, quoted in O'Brien, *Vince*, 303–4.

33. Kramer, *Instant Replay*, 196.

34. Ibid., quoted in O'Brien, *Vince*, 305.

35. Maraniss, *When Pride Still Mattered*, 384.

36. Ibid., 435.

37. Ibid., 460.

38. Ibid., 436.

39. Dowling, *Coach*, 288–89.

40. Wiebusch, *Lombardi*, 97.

41. Dowling, *Coach*, 287–88.

42. Wiebusch, *Lombardi*, 97.

43. Dowling, *Coach*, 212.

44. Ibid., 213.

45. Ibid., 64.

46. Ibid., 218.

47. Carroll, *When the Grass Was Real*, 40.

48. Dowling, *Coach*, 293–94.

49. Ibid., 130.

50. Ibid., 285.

51. Wiebusch, *Lombardi*, 44–45.

52. Dowling, *Coach*, 286.

53. Ibid., 296.

Chapter 5: Assorted Memories

1. O'Brien, *Vince*, 375.
2. Wiebusch, *Lombardi*, 16.
3. Ibid., 21.
4. Ibid., 32.
5. Ibid., 18.
6. Ibid., 15.
7. O'Brien, *Vince*, 182.
8. Ibid., 165.
9. Maraniss, *When Pride Still Mattered*, 313.
10. Wiebusch, *Lombardi*, 50.
11. Maraniss, *When Pride Still Mattered*, 342.
12. O'Brien, *Vince*, 185.
13. Wiebusch, *Lombardi*, 59.
14. Maraniss, *When Pride Still Mattered*, 356.
15. Ibid., 373.

Chapter 6: Lombardi Speaks Out

1. Vince Lombardi Jr., *What It Takes to Be #1: Vince Lombardi on Leadership* (New York: McGraw-Hill, 2001), 15.
2. O'Brien, *Vince*, 236.
3. Lombardi, *What It Takes to Be #1*, 161.
4. Briggs, *Strive to Excel*, 86.
5. Ibid., 87.
6. Dowling, *Coach*, 69.
7. Lombardi, *What It Takes to Be #1*, 255.
8. Ibid., 57.
9. Briggs, *Strive to Excel*, 121.
10. O'Brien, *Vince*, 61.
11. Ibid., 184.
12. Ibid., 203.
13. Ibid., 205–6.

14. Lombardi, *What It Takes to Be #1*, 26.
15. Ibid., 217.
16. Maraniss, *When Pride Still Mattered*, 215.
17. O'Brien, *Vince*, 139.
18. Maraniss, *When Pride Still Mattered*, 202.
19. O'Brien, *Vince*, 229.
20. Lombardi, *What It Takes to Be #1*, 67.
21. Maraniss, *When Pride Still Mattered*, 73.
22. O'Brien, *Vince*, 283.
23. Ibid., 177.
24. Lombardi, *What It Takes to Be #1*, 52.
25. Dowling, *Coach*, 30.
26. Maraniss, *When Pride Still Mattered*, 426.
27. Ibid., 424.
28. Lombardi, *What It Takes to Be #1*, 88.
29. O'Brien, *Vince*, 104.
30. Ibid., 199.
31. Vince Lombardi with W. C. Heinz, *Run to Daylight!* (New York: Grosset and Dunlap, 1963), 7.
32. Lombardi, *What It Takes to Be #1*, 202.
33. Lombardi, *Run to Daylight!* 11.
34. Maraniss, *When Pride Still Mattered*, 106.
35. Lombardi, *Run to Daylight!* 29.
36. Maraniss, *When Pride Still Mattered*, 165.
37. Ibid., 272.
38. Ibid., 273.
39. Lombardi, *Run to Daylight!* 47.
40. Briggs, *Strive to Excel*, 57.
41. Ibid., 65.
42. Lombardi, *Run to Daylight!* 73.
43. Briggs, *Strive to Excel*, 9.
44. Lombardi, *Run to Daylight!* 122.

45. O'Brien, *Vince*, 167.

46. Ibid.

47. Ibid.

48. Lombardi, *Run to Daylight!* 68.

49. O'Brien, *Vince*, 259.

50. Briggs, *Strive to Excel*, 24.

51. Lombardi, *Run to Daylight!* 149.

52. Maraniss, *When Pride Still Mattered*, 61.

53. Briggs, *Strive to Excel*, 112.

54. Lombardi, *Run to Daylight!* 186.

55. Maraniss, *When Pride Still Mattered*, 457.

56. O'Brien, *Vince*, 207.

57. Briggs, *Strive to Excel*, 29.

58. Ibid., 135.

59. O'Brien, *Vince*, 196.

60. Dowling, *Coach*, 73.

61. Ibid., 160.

62. Maraniss, *When Pride Still Mattered*, 497.

INDEX

Aldridge, Lionel, 119, 126
Amen, Paul, 26

Bengtson, Phil, 117
Blaik, Earl "Red," 20, 21, 25–26, 50
Bledsoe, Terry, 190
Bratkowski, Zeke, 106–7
Brown, Larry, 168, 171
Brown, Rosey, 83

Chance, Bill, 52–53, 61–62
Cochran, John "Red," 100
Conerly, Charlie, 66
Cosell, Howard, 183
Curry, Bill, 126

Danowski, Ed, 3, 16, 18, 21
Davis, Willie, 105, 125, 145–46, 219
DeGasperis, John, 8, 13–14
Dietzel, Paul, 26
Dowler, Boyd, 99–100, 108–10, 120–21, 144–45, 148–50, 157–58, 172

Elmblad, Bruce, 39

Fischer, Pat, 169–70, 171
Fleming, Marv, 220

Gifford, Frank, 66, 73, 74, 76, 81
Gillman, Sid, 21, 26, 37–39

Grabowski, Jim, 152
Green, Jack, 46
Green, John, 26
Gregg, Forrest, 94–95, 96–98, 101–2, 107, 111–13, 122, 143–44, 147, 162

Heap, Joe, 71
Hickman, Herman, 26
Higgins, Larry, 6–8, 10–12, 15–16, 18–20, 192–94, 195
Hornung, Paul, 111, 134, 135, 219
Howell, Jim Lee, 65, 73–74, 88
Huff, Sam, 72, 124–25, 198–99

Ice Bowl, the, 139–43, 146–50, 212

Jordan, Henry, 103, 118, 119
Jurgensen, Sonny, 164–65, 166

Kennedy, Ethel, 180
Koeppler, Jack, 199–200
Kramer, Jerry, 118, 126–27, 128, 133–35, 150

Landry, Tom, 65, 69, 70, 72, 73, 75, 84, 92, 138, 146–47
Lane, Chuck, 155
Lawlor, Jim, 16–17
Leahy, Frank, 71
Lilly, Bob, 115–17, 137, 141–43

Lodge, Jerry, 31–35, 55–56, 63–64
Lombardi, Joe, 4–5, 5–6, 9–10, 14–15
Lombardi, Marie, 104, 182
Lombardi, Vince, Jr., 54–55, 87–88, 89–90, 152–53, 156, 178, 180–81, 190–92, 200–201

MacAfee, Ken, 67–68, 70–71, 86
MacArthur, Douglas, 29, 59
Mack, Red, 132–33, 183–88
Mara, Wellington, 66, 88, 188–89
Maraniss, David, 37
Maule, Tex, 190
Maynard, Don, 77–81, 82
McGee, Max, 158–59, 189
Mercein, Chuck, 154–55, 157
Miller, Glenn, 153–54
Mischak, Robert, 76
Moore, Timothy, 5

Nitschke, Ray, 219–20
Nixon, Richard M., 179
Nolan, Dick, 66–67, 68, 84–86

Olejniczak, Dominic, 95

Paulekas, Al, 28–29, 30–31, 47, 62–63
Promuto, Vince, 164, 172

Reich, Gil, 40–42, 177–78
Remmel, Lee, 93–94, 98–99, 105–6, 124, 159–60, 162
Rich, Herb, 68

Richter, Pat, 160–61, 165, 166–68, 169
Robinson, Dave, 128–32, 141, 159, 182–83
Rollow, Cooper, 196
Rote, Kyle, 66, 71
Rozelle, Pete, 196–97

Sabol, Steve, 200
Schoenke, Ray, 135–36, 162–64
Schramm, Tex, 15–56, 83–84, 139–41, 174–77, 188
Seidell, Herbert, 20, 22–24
Seven Blocks of Granite, 16, 26, 45, 81
Skoronski, Bob, 108
Starr, Bart, 73, 113–14, 218–19
Starr, Ben, 154
Stone, Hardy, 45–46, 53, 62
Summerall, Pat, 82

Taylor, Jim, 95–96, 103–4, 107, 119, 122–23, 127–28, 138

Vann Peter, 35–37, 48–50, 57–60, 194–95, 197–98

Ward, Gene, 24
Warmath, Murray, 26, 37, 61
Williams, Travis, 221
Wycislo, Aloysius, 104

Yeoman, Bill, 26, 27–28, 42–45, 50–52, 60–61